Investment Economics & Risk

Levi Donohoe

Copyright © 2017 Levi Donohoe

All rights reserved.

ISBN: 1543191231
ISBN-13: 978-1543191233

To my late Grandfather Alan 'Jelly' Hills

Here's to another feather in my cap

'Formal education will make you a living; self-education will make you a fortune' - Jim Rohn

CONTENTS

Part 1 – Introduction
Formal Introduction....................................10

Part 2 – Investment Economics
Fallacy of composition 15
Zero Lower Bound Interest Rates & Creative Destruction 16
Value Added Tax and Household Saving Ratios.. 25
Debt Contracts-information asymmetry and credit rationing...27
Credit Rationing Model.............................30
Theory of Hysteresis....................................31
Property Investment Economics.......................33
The Perils of Government Statistics..................38
Economics of Pharmaceutical Industry................40
Patents and Innovation..............................45
The Lindy Effect....................................47
Inflation, the Output Gap & the curious case of Zimbabwe....50
Investing in Oligopolistic Industries...................53

Part 3 - Primary Commodities
What affects the price of commodities...............56
Commodity Producing Countries......................57
The Substitution Effect..............................59
Price Floors and the Shutdown Rule..................61
Dutch Disease and the Resource Trap................63
Other Sources of Dutch Disease......................66
Agriculture..69

Part 4 - Emerging Economies
Infant Industry Tariffs...............................75
The Race to The Bottom............................76
The Poverty Trap....................................77
Geography – The Landlocked Problem............. 78
The Demographic Dividend.........................81
The Importance of Foreign Direct Investment in

Underdeveloped Countries..84
Autocratic Economies..88
Rich Countries with Poor People..89

Part 5 – Capital Flows & Foreign Exchange
Capital Flows & Foreign Exchange..92
Global Liquidity..95
Currency Pegs..96
Fiscals Stimulus & Cross Border Money Flows....................100
Foreign exchange and Enterprise Risk................................102
Investing in Precious Metals..104
Efficient Market Hypothesis...109
Investment Cashflow...112
Central Banks and Foreign Exchange.................................115

Part 6 – Investment Risk
The Agency Problem..119
Hammurabi Law and Bank Nationalization..........................122
Risk in Overseas Investment..125
Portfolio Risk and Decisional Bias......................................127
The Endowment Effect..130
The Loss Aversion Theory...131
Winners Curse..132
The Survivorship Bias...133
Confirmation Bias...135
The Boiling Frog Syndrome...137
Bookmaker, Insurance and the Law of Large Numbers......138
Black Swan Events..139
Black Swan Problem & Oil Company Insurance Strategies..141
The Problem of Induction..144
Naïve Diversification and Risk Mitigation..........................145
Entering Emerging Markets – Risk....................................149
Joint Ventures and Acquisitions..153
Board of Directors and Risk Management..........................155
The Relationship Between Risk and Innovation..................157
The Success Breeds Failure Syndrome..............................160
Risk and Regulation..163

Part 7 - Closing Comments & Forecasts
Scenario Analysis...165
The Malthusian Trap...168
Entitlements Culture...170
Debt – An Economical Perspective..................................175
Statistical Inference...179
The Rise of China..181
China's Demographic Dividend..182
Solar – a Bright Future..184
Hope for the Future...187
The Future of the Oil Market...191
Graphene..195
How the West can be saved..197
Our Future World..202

References

'If I hadn't seen such riches I could live with being poor'
- James

ACKNOWLEDGMENTS

With thanks to my parents for their continued support over the years and to my Sophia for her encouragement when I needed it. These words would never have been written without you all

1

INTRODUCTION

In the aftermath of the financial crisis of 2008, whilst economists and market commentators were preaching financial Armageddon and tax payer's money was being used to prop up the financial sector, my father's heavy engineering company was celebrating making record profits. It occurred to me that whatever investors thought about the outlook of the economy, money never sleeps. Opportunities are constantly presenting themselves to those that are paying attention - all that is required is adequate foresight and an open mind.

I once had the pleasure of speaking with a student Doctor who was several months away from becoming qualified. During the discussion that we shared - he stated that after many years of study he felt that he had merely learned 'how not to kill patients'. He explained that if he could preserve life then there was every chance of healing a sick patient. I thought about this and realized that this shares parallels with economics and investing. If one can incorporate a high standard of economic theory into investment decisions then at the very least, principle can be preserved by the avoidance of poor investment decisions. By default, if one's portfolio is not depreciating then it should be appreciating.

The focus of this book is centralized upon financial risk and the economics of investment. By the very nature of interest in this field - investors will desire profits that exceed the general market's returns. It occurred to me that to realize better than average profits, one must be willing to think differently than other market participants. I realized that conventional economic books all seemed to discuss the same sort of topics; utility maximization, the Phillips Curve, overviews of fiscal and monetary policies as well as the division of labor theorem. Although important economic concepts - this was not going to allow me to experience above average returns especially as other investors are reading the same books. On the contrary, focus here will be given to paradigms of capital flows, foreign exchange and commodity price movements in addition to miscellaneous economic theories that evade attention of economic books aimed toward the general public and retail investors. Only topics that bare significance in investment decisions and portfolio risk management are included in this book.

After completing my Economics and Mathematics degree, I was left with more questions than answers.

- Could Africa become the next 'China'?

- How can countries like Venezuela with world class oil reserves be so poor?

- How are companies impacted by FX movements?

- What should I look for when selecting individual equities?

To answer these questions, I frequently found myself studying a wide range of literature and studies as part of my own self-interest and in satisfying some of the research projects on my Master's degree in Risk. It dawned on me that I had studied so much empirical and theoretical papers that if concatenated with my own views on the world, would make an excellent read for fellow enthused investors.

I became critical of the economic theories that endorsed policies utilized by central banks - not necessarily accepting the claims made at face value. The reader will note this as being a constant theme throughout all of the featured chapters. The importance of independent thinking has never been as important to me as it is today and I have incorporated this critical analysis into the content of this book.

The development of globalization has changed the economic playing field and the power of old that central banks held on economic output is diminishing. I believe it is imperative for economic theory to be revised and refined as developments in the global economy alter what we know about what we think we know about the world.

Our current era is an important and fascinating one; never before have so many economies been so weak at the same time. Asset valuations are disconnected from the fundamentals of the assets that they are supposedly reflecting. With lofty asset valuations it can be difficult to search for value in the markets. However, as you will learn from the content disclosed herein; with the liquidity in the global markets, no matter how inflated assets appear or how poor prospects seem to be, there will always be a bull market in some asset class somewhere in the world. This ensures that there will be capacity for profiteering, if one knows what to look for of course.

If by accident more than design, the theory and empirical observations detailed within this book are fashioned in a way that their applicability will not recede with time. Basic economic concepts will be bypassed as more than enough books have been written on these subjects. This no-nonsense account is very to the point and only details theory that will be of interest to the investment community.

When I first decided to write a book, I wondered which specialty to focus on. With a background of Economics, Mathematics and Risk - the content of any book that I authored could be extremely pliable. As you will observe, this book neglects to adhere to any particular specialty. Instead, it offers a collage of theories that can be utilized in making investment decisions and to decipher the global economy. And so, I present this book to you with the mindset that if one single book could be sent back in time to my former self when I first became interested in investing - it would be this one.

2

INVESTMENT ECONOMICS

The Fallacy of Composition

An interesting notion in economics is the assumption error in actions that benefit at an individual level must also hold throughout the economy. A renowned example of this being a concept coined as the 'paradox of thrift'. This occurs when individuals decide to increase their savings but it fails to lead to a subsequent increase in aggregate savings for the entire economy. On an individual level, the increase in thriftiness can be funneled into investments which can support consumption at a later date, this, in itself, being a positive endeavor.

Understanding that your spending is my income and my spending is someone else's income will aid in understanding this misconception. If on aggregate everyone in the economy decided to save more - it would lead to a dramatic reduction in spending activities and would cause a subsequent fall in aggregate demand and rise in joblessness. Whilst on an individual basis making savings or repayments against debts would result in a better self-assessment, if the entire economy paid down debts in concert it could tip the economy into recession. Subsequently policy makers have adopted approaches that encourage credit fueled consumption rather than rewarding the misers.

It is the link between consumer spending and economic growth that policy makers have attempted to exploit in order to kick start the economy. Holding interest rates at artificially low levels are said to increase the propensity for households to consume and businesses to invest. If this is the case, then why did central banks hold interest rates at zero lower bound for a near decade and the economy react with negligible growth?

Zero Lower Bound Interest Rates & Creative Destruction

Basic economic concepts will be avoided herein, however, the interest rate mechanism is central to the comprehension of the content throughout this book and so a brief summary will be given for convenience.

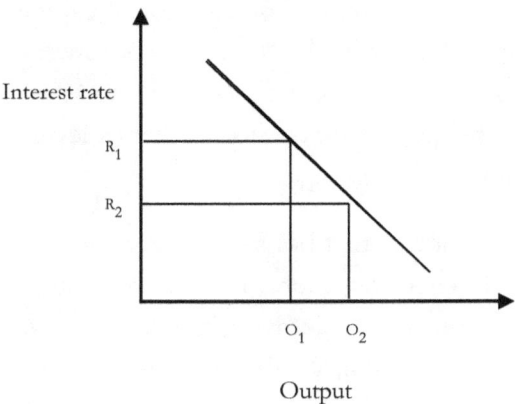

The above figure illustrates the saving and investment curve with its negative gradient showing equilibrium points for any given interest rate. At interest rate R_1 (let's say represents 5%) the corresponding output is given as o_1. If the interest rate is reduced to R_2 (4% for example) then the output shifts rightward to o_2, representing a higher level of output in the economy. The model suggests that the interest rate can be manipulated to titrate the amount of output within an economy. If, at o_2, the economy is becoming febrile with inflation escalating - the central bank can increase the interest rate to R_1 which will curtail output as desired.

A rise in interest rates will increase the cost of capital and also reward the miser rather than the consumer – these conditions will increase the propensity to save. In sum, the exchange rate mechanism acts as a lever on consumption and savings.

Conventional economic text books will detail how low interest rates encourage investment in projects and expansion of aggregate demand, thus in turn, boosting economic growth. Whilst this may hold in some circumstances, how does one explain the stagnant growth seen whilst interest rates have been reduced to zero for a near decade? Is the entire western hemisphere that innately weak that interest rates cannot be raised with stimulus inducing policies rendered impotent?

Holding interest rates at, or immediately above zero in the medium to long term is a form of protectionism. Japan gained significant criticism when it supported its 'zombie firms'. That is, propping up companies that are otherwise uncompetitive in the view of buoying employment levels within the economy. Holding interest rates at zero lower bound is effectively creating the same effect. It is supporting firms that may not be able to remain profitable under what can be deemed as 'normal conditions' of higher interest rates as determined by market forces. By creating an environment of fiscal and monetary policies that provide life support to inefficient firms - less new entrants may be entering the market and capital allocation from banks may not be distributed to companies with the most optimal growth prospects – resulting in a misallocation of capital that may foster new growth.

The central bank's policy of holding interest rates low seems to be maximizing employment and hoping that diverting capital into asset markets will generate wealth that will duly trickle down into the real economy. However, holding interest rates at zero lower bound is preventing the creative destruction process and is arguably a large reason why growth in the Western hemisphere has been stagnant. Surviving is not the same as thriving. Many companies have issued profit warnings and resorted to 'internal devaluations' in which employees have accepted salary reductions or paucity increases in order to remain competitiveness with dated business models.

In my view, central banks will hold interest rates below the rate of inflation for the foreseeable future, this being an effective tax on capital deposits and encourages credit driven consumption. Interestingly, the interest rate mechanism has not always been regarded as a tool to manipulate output. In the wake of the Weimar hyperinflation crisis in Germany – many of the Reischbank members considered that a rise in interest rates would increase the cost of production and therefore promote price inflation[1].

Creative destruction is an economic theory that intimates that recessions and crisis may be necessary for sustained economic growth. A new market will grow after an innovation. Often this will induce imitators to enter and eventually erode the original pioneer's profit margins by competition, causing the market to stagnate. Recessions are an important way of rebooting the economy - by clearing the deadwood and allowing for new growth. When a recession occurs and unemployment rises, it provides an incentive for unemployed entrepreneurs to adapt and take risks. This business cycle has repeated throughout history and has been a vital ingredient in our development. Except now we have a group of academics in control of central banks that believe they can tame business cycles by manipulating interest rates and tempering the money supply. These policies that have attempted to smooth the economic cycles have actually exacerbated them with increased volatility leading to higher booms and deeper busts.

Additionally, with the ushering of liquidity into capital assets - we should not overlook the fact that volatility will often increase with an appreciation in the asset's price. A 2% adjustment on a £1 stock is a $\pm$ 2 pence per share movement. Whereas the same percentage oscillation with a £15 stock is $\pm$ 30 pence per share.

This fluctuation represents the same relative change but it is much more pronounced in the latter example. One can determine that volatility will appear to be increasing linearly with the market's appreciation. Such wild swings can provoke more emotion from market participants as movements appear more dramatic than they actually are. This is an important consideration in the property market given the high valuations. One can imagine the emotion of leveraged property investors if home prices fell by a mere 5%. Nevertheless, it is best for central banks and governments to refrain from intervening in the free markets. Their spurious actions distort everything and cause one intervention to lead to another. Many economists agree that this is exactly what happened between market peaks of 2000 and 2008.

The policy response from the dot-com bubble was to reduce interest rates. This loosening of monetary policy increased the pool of liquidity which made it possible for capital to flow into the housing market, in turn creating untenable prices. When the market crashed in 2008 the response was to reduce interest rates further. It is perceivable that this has led to unsustainably high prices in all major asset markets. Stocks, real estate, classic cars, art markets and bonds are all near all-time highs. The only asset class to be at historic lows are currencies. The injection of liquidity into the system has created asset bubbles across the board which are increasing the risk of an asset price deflation crash- maybe not in concert but one should question the sustainability of these valuations. The central banks may be able to prop up several asset classes but it is unlikely that they will be able to sustain all of these markets in tandem over a prolonged period.

My personal recommendation is to raise interest rates. It will invariably cause weaker companies to collapse and unemployment will rise, asset prices will fall and some people will lose their money but inertia at this stage will only increase the burden on the tax payer in the future. It will also incentivize innovation. A great criticism of central banks is the refusal to accept some short term pain in order to pave way for a better future. Attempts to iron out economic cycles is an obvious prodrome and will not end well, the question at this time is when and how. The scale of intervention that we have seen in the market will not lead to a smooth pathway to prosperity.

Allowing the creative destruction process to occur is a necessary evil to create new growth and increase propensity for entrepreneurs to innovate. Some analysts propose that the process of change is often slow and incremental until a crisis develops, thus bringing about significant and rapid change. On balance of this evidence, a crisis could provide the necessary conditions to break out of the current stagnant growth. However, the realization of a crisis may not be essential to create propensity to change - expectations of a crisis may be a sufficient catalyst to invoke change. Pre-emptive coping or evasive strategies are in essence both strategic changes and risk strategies[2] . The Central Bank's attempts to distort labor market cycles may be reducing the incentive for individuals to innovate and take risk.

In the UK, general elections are held every five years. This encourages an element of 'short-termism' in which governments focus on preventing crisis occurring on their watch. No party wants to be the one that raised interest rates and caused people to lose their jobs. Even if this is a necessary requirement for a more prosperous future. It is much more desirable for governments to treat symptoms when they occur rather than tackle the underlying causes. This may aid in explaining why interest rates were not raised when the economy started to show signs of improvement in 2011. It was an opportunity to revert back to more normalized conditions but was not capitalized on.

Zero lower bound interest rates causes a loss of purchasing power and encourages inflation of asset prices as investors pile into capital assets to preserve wealth. A negative real interest rate is a hidden tax on capital deposits. This is an important consideration as with a mere two per cent rate of inflation, capital that yields no interest would half in value every thirty-five years. At the time of writing, the world economy is in unchartered territory in respect to many of the western economies entering their ninth year of zero lower bound interest rates. Whether this mechanism has aided economic growth is unproven and far from certain. Positive real interest rates provide savers with an income, the insurance and pension fund industries also rely on interest rate yields for cashflow. Due to the lack of return on investment for savers, it remains to be seen whether meagre yields encourage consumption or if the saving ratio increases in an effort to offset the lack of capital growth. Any excess capital could be used to pay down debts rather than invest due to the disparity between interest rates on mortgages and the yield offered by savings accounts.

Should the households that are saving for retirement become anxious about lack of interest payments - it is conceivable that they will respond by saving more. What's more, by reducing the return of conventional safe investments, savers are forced to invest in riskier prospects in the search of yield. It should be very clear that by reducing interest rates to their current level you are forcing people to speculate in order to capture a return on their capital. The objective of reducing interest rates is to divert the flow of capital from saving instruments into consumption activities within the economy.

Intuitively then, one must question the purpose of conflating two counteracting policies of zero lower bound interest rates which are designed to facilitate consumer spending but the application of a 20% value added tax on products in the consumer market - make goods more expensive.

Value Added Tax and Household Saving Ratios

When one first studies the Keynesian approach to economics they could question the use of Value Added Tax (VAT). Keynes once jested that the government should pay workers to dig holes and then fill them back in again as the wages from such activities would be spent in other businesses within the economy and cause a wave of employment underpinned by consumption. From this, the multiplier effect was coined and is still a vital component of economic analysis today.

After the 2008 credit crisis governments have been participating in large scale public spending provisions in order to create demand in their domestic economies, in turn, creating indirect employment. After all, your spending is my income as is my spending someone else's income. This is an important policy as economies can naturally reside at low employment equilibriums and government intervention is often a necessity to encourage consumption and economic activity. The paradox of thrift shows us that a sudden stop of consumer spending will swiftly coincide with a wave of unemployment.

One must, on this basis, question the role of VAT which is applied to many goods and services in the UK. Surely the application of a 20% tax is counteractive to the fiscal policies governments are committed to? The explanation to this paradox lies with the household saving ratio. By applying a 20% tax, governments can receive funds that may have been saved by households as investments, therefore allowing the government to spend what otherwise would have been saved. Tax increases can be used to shape patterns of consumption. If the economy was nearing a recession, the very mention of a rise in tax applied to goods may cause people to bring forward their consumption and make the purchase(s) before any anticipated rise in pricing. In turn allowing the economy to avert a recession.

Conversely, if the economy appears to be 'overheating' a rise in tax can taper consumption and bring the economy back to any given equilibrium trend. This is an example of an economic stabilizer. The other stabilizer being unemployment benefits that are issued to job seekers or agents that are otherwise unemployed. Although these sorts of benefits have a negative stigma attached to them, they are an important stabilizer in the economy as individuals that do not have any other income will be able to consume and make some contribution to demand within the economy. The government supplementing consumption makes sense in certain conditions, however, injecting this capacity into the banking system has resulted in a clear misallocation of capital that has not boosted the real economy. Debt contracts under a typical information asymmetry can show how this capital has led to a misallocation of capital by not being distributed to the agents that need it the most.

Debt Contracts – Information Asymmetry and Credit Rationing

Since the 2008 financial crash, banking stocks have performed relatively badly to other sectors of the global economy. Economic theory can show an inherent weakness in the debt contract process between small and medium enterprises (SME) and the banks. If investing in a SME, availability of credit is an extremely important consideration. SMEs can be reliant on securing external funding whereas a multinational company could use retained profits to fund new ventures.

A conventional debt contract will involve the SME repaying the principle of the loan plus interest, the danger for the bank is that the SME becomes insolvent before indemnifying the principle - leaving the bank with a loss. There is an opportunity for the firm borrowing the debt due to the reward structure of these types of agreements. If the project is successful, then the SME can repay the principle and retain any profit generated from the project funded with the bank loan. If the venture fails and the loan is not repaid, the losses are divided between the borrower and the bank.

If one accepts the trade-off between risk and reward, it is conceivable that in the pursuit of high profits; firms may be induced to undertake high risk ventures with an elevated chance of failure. The bank would rather lend to an enterprise that is able to repay the capital borrowed irrespective of project risk. Therefore, there is a divergence of preferences as the bank would rather only finance lower risk projects that offer a likelihood of success and consequential repayment of the principle.

Information asymmetry can distort this process as the bank will find it difficult to differentiate between projects that are of a high risk nature and those of lower risk. A factor exacerbating this being that once the funds are transferred to the debtor, the bank has no control over how the funds are spent. A remedy for this information asymmetry could be to set the default interest rate higher to offset any defaults on high risk projects as the profit generated on successful repayments will offset defaults.

This has potential to lead to an adverse selection problem in which low risk low reward projects that would otherwise be able to repay principle plus interest would be priced out of the market and forced to seek other methods of raising capital. Put simply, by raising the interest rates for all projects, the bank will be funding more higher risk projects which invariably lead to them lending to more projects that are destined to fail. If a high risk project is successful, the debtor can retain all profits whilst the bank has a fixed return irrespective of the amount of capital the project generated.

In an environment of information asymmetry, economic theory suggests that the optimal solution for the bank would be to limit the supply of loans.

The Credit Rationing Model

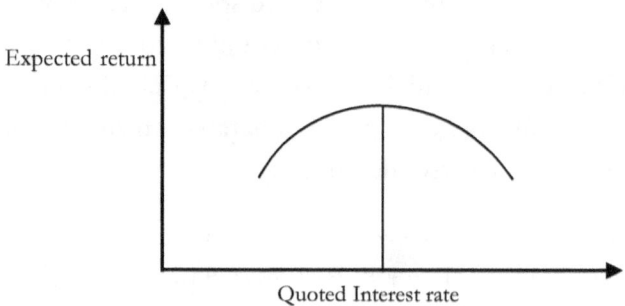

The above model shows the return to the bank under an information asymmetry as interest rates are increased to find an optimum rate of interest. The bank's expected income increases with the interest rate for lower rates. Showing that the bank can increase profitability by increasing interest rates. This holds until the vertical line interception with the gradient becoming zero. Here, the bank's expected yield decreases as the interest rate is increased. The justification for this being that the higher interest charges are attracting less low risk projects and so there is a higher proportion of borrowers defaulting which reduces the profitability of the bank. Optimal interest rates are found where the gradient of the curve is zero. Below this, profits can be increased with a rise in interest rates. Beyond this, profits fall due to an increase in debtors failing as only high risk high reward ventures will be tempted by the high interest rate charge. The solution is to ration the amount of loans at the interest rate that provides a stationary point on the credit rationing model. The bank will be able to determine this point by their profits and losses on loans. Banks lending to new business ventures require accurate risk pricing to establish the project's value. If the debtor defaults then any remaining assets can be liquidated to recuperate funds lost by the bank, in many circumstances the assets may have paltry resale value. Yet, with real-estate, the bank will be able to sell this for the market price which is often relatively predictable. So, it seems that in terms of risk tolerance - favoring the issuance of credit against brick and mortar rather than other types of investment is a risk assessing sanctuary for lenders. This illustrates why much of the newly created purchasing power by the banking system meant to underpin consumption has found its way into the real estate markets.

The Theory of Hysteresis

The theory of hysteresis articulates that equilibriums in the economy depend on what has occurred in the past. The theory is often referred to in the labor markets in which current unemployment levels are a function of unemployment levels of past. This theory holds for numerous reasons, the more prominent ones being that workers that are unemployed lose the ability to develop or maintain their human capital, that is, their ability to maintain and update their skill set through working practices. Faced with a high unemployment environment, it can be difficult for talented workers to prove their worth by occupying jobs and gaining promotion. This, arguably, may lead to inefficiencies which in turn reduces the aggregate demand for labor.

Given that some workers successfully retain their employment status during unemployment shocks, it is proposed that this strengthens their wage bargaining power and so commands of higher wages are made. An asymmetry is said to emerge in which market participants enjoy an increase in wage bargaining power and inversely, inactive workers lose their ability to influence wage setting policies. With higher wages afforded to existing workers, aggregate wages per se increase and with it unemployment levels escalate. In an environment of negligible wage increases and strong housing markets, property investors should focus on the apparent decoupling of wage and house inflation.

It is often considered that elevating unemployment is a symptom of workers receiving salaries in excess of what they should be receiving, paying ourselves more than we deserve. In this view one could say that when the government tells us that the economy is strong because there are record levels of employment; could this be because workers are employed for less than their worth? I accept employment levels are high but the quality of jobs has fallen markedly. If this view is accepted, one must consider there a trade of with quantity and quality of jobs in the market. Employment may have increased but the increase has been largely in the services sector which are generally poor quality jobs.

Traditionally a rise in unemployment would result in a fall in wages, allowing workers to price themselves back into the market at a lower wage equilibrium than before. In the absence of a robust increase in wages, one must question the sustainability of house price inflation.

Property Investment

Investors have been infatuated with the property market for as long as living memory can recall. There is a significant proportion of wealth tied into the property markets. Most of the richest well-to-do families in the world acquired wealth through investing in portfolios of property. Whether this is ascribed to sound investment dexterity or because they did not do anything more stupid with their money is debatable. After all, some people are much better at making money than others and so if a young adult inherits their wealthy grandparents estates – having this money parked into property has been a good way to preserve wealth, there would have been multiple opportunities to lose the lot in stock market boom and bust cycles. The property market has acted as a platform for wealth generation and as a vehicle for intergenerational wealth relay.

In today's market, the main challenge of breaking away from zero lower bound interest rates is that the amount of leverage in the system is an indicator of the economy's vulnerability to an interest rate rise. The media has a tendency to fixate our attention on any small gyration of property prices but the problem is not if the housing markets falls by 10% - the problem is the leverage in the market. If you own your house outright and do not have a mortgage you shouldn't be too concerned if the house price goes down by 10% or up by 15% as it is still the same house. If, for instance, you finance your house purchase with 125% credit with the expectation that the price of the house will continue to appreciate allowing you to pay off the principle owed when selling the house – that is where the problem is.

The property investors that have previously purchased various houses on margin will have done very well in the bull markets but they also stand to lose the most in any market correction. Because of the flooding of liquidity into the system, I imagine that consumer price inflation will at some stage accelerate and house prices will deflate in real terms. Let's imagine home prices appreciate say 3 or 4 percent in nominal terms and the rate of inflation is 6% then obviously you have a depreciation in real terms of 2-3% per annum. This is a very feasible scenario, I envisage that the property market will endure some sort of correction but maybe only in real terms.

An excellent early warning signal in any asset class is that a colossal rise in prices that is underpinned by an increase in credit should be viewed with great caution. There has been a divergence between wage growth and house prices for some time in the UK. Unless the gains realized in the property market trickle down into wage inflation then one may struggle to envisage a scenario in which house prices can continue their price trend seen in recent years. This scenario will lead to a proportionate reduction in rent yields to property prices. Raising the minimum wage will help to underpin house price inflation but salaries will need to outperform respective gains in house prices or the leverage in the system will need to expand further.

A theme in the last decade is that a substantial amount of capital has been invested in the housing market as capital chases yield. I would be extremely cautious of being overweight property as paper profits are precarious and contingent on central bank policies favoring the continued underpinning of asset prices. It also assumes that the central bank is capable of supporting house prices in adverse conditions. In my view, the amount of leverage in the housing market will act as a deadweight on future interest rate hikes because the increases in mortgage debt repayments will significantly impact the working class.

As the Bank of England has indicated, we should become accustomed to a new lower equilibrium interest rate which is largely a function of the leveraged debt in the system. It is reasonable to be concerned with the limitations of controlling inflation if interest rates are contained to protect the lofty property market and its highly geared owners. Usually policy makers would hike interest rates to starve off inflation but this will increase mortgage payments at a time where wage growth has been flat - thus eroding disposable income. After 1997 in Hong Kong house prices fell by 70% but none of the major developers went bankrupt and very few households went into foreclosure[3]. The reason for this being chiefly because the level of debts in the system were much lower than those seen when the housing market collapsed in 2008.

The paradigm of reductions in the typical homeowner's equity relative to the price of property has caused excessive leverage which politicians seem to neglect to mention in build up to elections. In fact, governments in the UK have pioneered policies to buoy house price inflation such as 'help to buy' schemes. This is emblematic of the three generation mortgage innovation in Japan in the late 1980s which was introduced to allow households to borrow funds that had repayment periods of up to 100 years[4]. In essence, an individual would agree to a loan that their grandchildren would eventually inherit liability for. Instead of recognizing that the gains in the housing market has become a bubble - lets create a financial product that propels it even higher.

When house prices are reported in nominal terms I want to make clear that this is a very limited indicator of value and can skew assumptions on the pricing of this asset class. Assessing whether the property market is becoming febrile or depressed should factor in more indicators before a hypothesis is accepted. A reliable, but by no means comprehensive approach is to assess the ratio between house prices and median salaries. Any deviation from the historic trend should be considered significant. Additionally, house prices measured in ounces of Gold is another indicator that can show if house prices are historically depressed or expensive. This features calculating how many ounces of Gold are required to purchase the average house.

Some of the biggest losses can be incurred by investing in markets deemed to be 'safe' and stable. Just because the housing market has performed relatively well over the past few decades does not mean that this will continue indefinitely. Property is not insulated from market forces that other asset classes are subjected to. Very few people predicted the crash in oil prices in late 2014 - no market is immune to market forces, including the property market. However, on balance, it is probable that home prices continue to rise in nominal terms but begin to depreciate in real terms – most people will be totally unaware of this due to their focus on nominal valuations and the fact that governments do not accurately report the rates of true inflation within an economy.

The Perils of Government Statistics

I once read a statement suggesting that the more an individual reads the news the less he knows about the world. At the time, I believed this was absurd and could not relate to the underlying message. With the passage of time I found that this paradoxical statement has significant merit. As my knowledge of economics expanded - I noticed the media would report very trifling matters and make quite extreme one-dimensional conclusions from it. A prime example being inflation reporting. The Consumer Price Index (CPI) is one of the main mechanisms to measure inflation in the economy, however, inflation is always higher than official reports suggest and so valuing asset prices from inaccurate data can result in significant misjudgments. As the famous actor Denzil Washington once said, 'if you don't read the newspaper you are uninformed, if you do read it you are misinformed'. One should view news reports with a curious suspicion and always gather information from more than one source due to ulterior motives of media corporations. The build up to the EU referendum in the UK highlighted just how filtered the news stations are in the UK. They had a heavy emphasis on reporting imperious 'remain' bias mantras and was very anti-Brexit throughout the campaign. It is possible that this only incentivized voters to rebel in the way that they did in the voting booths.

In regards to inflation, the CPI measures the change in prices of a basket of commodities over time. If the aggregate price change is +1.2% then inflation is given as 1.2% for the specified time period. However, if a product such as orange juice increases by 5%, orange juice could be removed from the basket and substituted with another good such as apple juice. The justification being that consumers would note the price increase and substitute it for a similar but cheaper good. This is how inflation will always be understated, any price increases are pushed to one side as the analyst deems appropriate. By switching products to be measured, a desired lower rate of inflation can be calculated. Weights are applied to the constituents of the basket and adjusted to suit which is open to further manipulation. This is seldom mentioned in the news reports.

The Economics of the Pharmaceutical Industry

To truly comprehend the allure of investing in pharmaceutical companies, a brief commentary of monopoly theory will be necessary. Thereafter, it will be evident why any stock portfolio should contain some exposure to this sector.

The main distinction between a firm in perfect competition and a monopolist is the firm is a 'price taker' whereas the monopolist is a 'price maker'. The market has set a price for the firm's produce and the firm has liberty to adjust output accordingly. If a firm attempted to sell its goods at a higher price than its competitors - demand would shift in favor of the cheaper goods supplied by other enterprises. A monopolist, conversely, has the ability to manipulate market price or the quantity to be supplied to the market. It cannot, however, set both as the market will determine the price of the goods given the quantity of goods supplied to market, or if the monopolist sets the price - the quantity will be determined by how many units consumers want at that specified price. By reducing its output, the monopolist can command a higher price. An obvious example of this being a large sovereign oil producer such as Saudi Arabia. Obversely, expanding output and flooding the market will lead to a reduction in price per unit. As more goods become available their cost will gradually fall.

A natural monopoly is said to exist if because of economies of scale, a large single operator in a market can supply the market at a lower average cost than can be achieved by a number of smaller companies. This being the most cost-efficient way of supplying goods to the market. A pure monopoly exists when a single firm is the only supplier of a market. It is this to which will be the focus of this section.

The reference to monopolies is important to comprehend as the pharmaceutical sector is riddled with monopolies. Here lies the coercion of investing in this sector. The industry itself is very capital intensive with R&D being a necessity to innovate new molecules. The reward for a company that achieves a breakthrough being exclusivity of selling the molecule under patent protection. Allowing the incumbent firm to charge monopoly prices for the drug that they have developed. If the lay person was asked to guess the most profitable industry in the immediate decades leading up to the millennia; one may excuse them for neglecting to consider the Pharmaceutical industry. Per the Organisation for Economic Co-operation and Development, the pharmaceutical industry ranked first or second in 24 out of the 32 years between 1960 and 1991 in Fortune magazine's ranking of the most profitable sectors in the US[5].

The pharmaceutical sector is composed of mainly large multinational companies (MNCs). Interestingly, R&D intensive companies often have lower levels of debt than firms in other industries as debt financing tends to not be used for riskier economic activities like molecule development trials. The composition of the sector and how this may change overtime will undoubtedly determine which companies outperform relative to rival syndicates. As aforementioned, the sector is dominated by large MNCs, a small amount of investigation can determine why this is the case. Larger MNCs have easier access to funding and can absorb losses incurred by writing off budding drugs that transpire to be subpar to minimalistic standards.

Patents typically offer the innovator exclusive producing rights for a period of twenty years which grants them a series of mini-monopolies. It has been observed that some of the larger enterprises have merged because of expected excess capacity in anticipation of patent expiry without sufficient replacements in the pipeline. Likewise, small and medium enterprises have merged in response to financial problems. Although not a fool proof strategy, one should view mergers with caution. Mergers may be in response to an underlying financial issue but to respond in this manner is certainly not a solution and investors should view mergers in the

Pharmaceutical markets with great suspicion.

One consideration that must not be overlooked when investing in pharmaceutical related companies is the status of current patents. Upon expiry of a patent the loss of revenue is severe. When the patent protection of Ciprofloxacin expired, generics entered the market causing the price to decline by 90%[6]. The time lapse to bring a new molecule to market tends to differ dependent on which report one reads, however, the dominant view of the industry is that it takes 10-12 years to develop a new molecule. It is obvious that the prospects of a pharmaceutical company are inextricably linked to the status of the patents which it owns. This said, there are some very successful generic manufacturing companies listed on stock exchanges however they do not enjoy the supernormal profits of patent holders.

Monopolistic markets can be extremely lucrative for any firm that manages to breach the monopoly and capture market share. This is important for two reasons, if investing in a firm that occupies a monopoly of a given market, a new market entrant can significantly reduce profit for the monopolist because the supernormal profits that they have accrued in the past will allow the new entrant to capture market share swiftly, thus incentivizing the monopolist to dramatically reduce prices. Secondly, any companies that manage to enter the market can receive short term profits in marked excess of normal business operations so the reward of achieving this is very attractive.

Gazprom enjoyed a monopoly of the gas supply to several Baltic countries via a network of pipelines, after all, it made economic sense for them to do so given the close proximity and the large natural gas reserves they have in Russia. Additionally, the cost of implementing the gas pipelines would be borne by Gazprom and under normal conditions there would be no reason for diversification of gas supply into the Baltic countries. However, Gazprom is 51% state owned and was tempering the supply of gas to these markets for political leverage[7]. Consequently, the price of gas in these countries was determined by Gazprom whom frequently abused their position for political reasons. Such market power permitted Gazprom to increase the price of gas dramatically when they decided to reduce supply. The fracking revolution allowed for the transportation of vast liquid natural gas reserves from the USA by sea to markets that was previously solely supplied by Gazprom. This action has reduced Gazprom's ability to fix prices in these markets and serves as a stark warning for any monopolistic company that abuses their position that they could be incentivizing activism from new entrants.

Patents and Innovation

Whether patents facilitate or retard innovation has been a debate amongst economists for some time. Some argue that due to the costs involved in R&D activities that they will be conducted by a firm on the condition that it can enjoy monopoly prices in the event of a breakthrough. If a company aspires to achieve an innovation that requires £2 million in investment, the successful technology could be imitated by rival companies and so the imitators can benefit as much as the innovator without incurring the R&D costs. Such free riding activities could reduce the incentive to engage in R&D as no company will want to fund an innovation the whole market can benefit from as much as they do. This is because once the innovation is known to competitors - the marginal cost of imitation is relatively very low.

In the absence of a willing pioneer, a standoff may ensue in which investment in innovation may be subdued or non-existent. What is important to recognize in this debate is that the patent process concerns commercialization of an innovative concept or new knowledge, basic research is not a function of patent policy as it goes on regardless as science actively seeks new knowledge. It is the commercial exploitation of the findings that may be reliant upon patent protection. The composition of the market will bear influence on the R&D intensity as a competitive firm has more to gain from innovative practices than a monopolist. This is because the competitive firm is situated in a position in which profitability may be non-existent, whilst a monopolist will be profiting handsomely from existing technology and so has little reasoning to change processes.

Not all theorists subscribe to the notion that patents are an essential ingredient of the innovation process. Some claim that strong Intellectual Property Rights (IPRs) constrain further technical progress by precluding other inventors from making similar inventions due to risk of infringement. This is an important consideration as the industrial revolution did not really materialize until Watt's patent expired in 1785, possibly as others were prevented from developing new models of steam engine until after this period due to fear of breaching the patent protection.

Opposition of patents claim that discovery and development would have occurred without the framework of patenting, as the pursuit of new knowledge and firms attempting to gain a competitive edge over others in the market would stimulate innovation. Perhaps the need for patent protection is more prominent in some sectors than others. From a macro perspective, patents can foster inequality within the global economy as the majority of countries need to imitate first before developing the capacity to innovate themselves. Strong patent and IPRs prevent the process of imitation and experimentation of existing technologies which is a crucial stage leading to subsequent innovation.

The Lindy Effect

Investing in technology centric enterprises demonstrates a very intricate balance of risk and reward as profits surge after an innovative breakthrough yet companies that fail to transit with new developments can quickly be left behind. There has been many examples of companies that have dominated market shares of sectors and within two years gone bust. The investor can do well to acknowledge the Lindy Effect when making assumptions on existing technology.

Benoit Mandelbrot, a renowned mathematician coined the expression 'Lindy Effect' and its applicability is best suited to forecasting the life expectancy of a non-perishable goods such as a technology. Mandelbrot posits that the current life term of an idea or technology is proportionate to its current age. That is, if an invention has been in existence for one year then pertaining to probability - the invention should survive an additional year. This is not to say that the technology will cease to exist in one year, it is an indicator that the technology is always approximately equal to the halfway point of its lifespan.

This, of course being dynamic and not static. If the above invention survives an extra month it will project an expectation of an additional year and one month of existence. The true merit of the Lindy Effect is to suggest that a technology that has stood the test of time is better positioned to survive in the future than one that has an unproven and emerging nature.

This holds for companies too. Whilst a company that was founded one hundred years ago may be expected to operate for a further one hundred years; we know from observation that a one hundred year company could become insolvent several months from now. What we can derive from this theory is that a company that has operated for three years from streaming videos online and receiving advertising revenue will likely continue for another three years minimum. Whereas a company that has manufactured solar panels for fifteen years will likely continue for a further fifteen years. This provides a very basic assumption on investing in technological centric enterprises.

If an entrepreneur could establish a company that made devices featuring virtual pets such as the 'Tamagotchi' fad in the late 1990s, or to manufacture standard calculators, the entrepreneur could be tempted to capitalize on the trend of young adults purchasing the Tamagotchi devices. However, if entering this market one year after the first devices were brought to market, the estimated timespan of the devices being a projection of a further year. Whilst handheld calculators originated in the 1970s. The Lindy Effect would suggest that over the medium term, calculators would be the better investment choice as this technology had a longer life projection than the Tamagotchi device.

If one accepts the notion of the Lindy Effect, it can be employed as a forecasting tool in which assumptions about the future are dependent on the age span of current technologies. If predicting the status of technological markets in a decade from now, one could assume that any technologies that have been pioneered in the last ten years will, in their current form, exist for up to a further ten years. Tinkering with improvements to the existing technology will duly increase the probability of the given technology surviving the test of time.

Inflation, the Output Gap and the Curious Case of Zimbabwe

Many theorists have participated to the attempts of modelling inflation from an economical perspective. Publications vary from explanations of inflation lags to output gaps. Interestingly, not one reference was made to the quantity of money supply and its influence on domestic pricing during the modules I studied as part of my economics degree.

Emphasis was made on aggregate demand and how inflation being putative to the level of output within an economy. With productivity acting as a tempering mechanism to control inflation. If inflation is excessive then increasing taxes or interest rates can taper consumption, on the contrary, reducing interest rates and initiate government spending to increase aggregate demand to warn off deflation. The output gap is employed to demonstrate exactly how policy makers can target inflation. The output gap being the difference between actual and equilibrium levels of demand. It follows that inflation, given as 'π', can be mathematically modelled by the following formula:

$$\pi = \pi^L + \alpha(Y - Y^e)$$

Inflation being a function of inflation in the previous period π^L plus the output gap's coefficient α which changes the importance of the output gap, which is denoted by $(Y - Y^e)$. This being the actual level of output minus the equilibrium output. If actual output (Y) is inferior to the equilibrium output (Y^e) then the output gap will be negative. If the actual output is greater than the equilibrium output then the output gap is positive and will provide an inflationary effect.

Intuition would suggest that in the event of a zero output gap inflation would be constant whilst a positive output gap causes inflation to increase. In a positive output gap workers are able to bargain for higher wages as firms translate this into price increases of produce. This process will continue indefinitely providing that the output gap is positive.

My thoughts are that economists endorsing this theory as a valid explanation of inflation levels within the economy should discuss this with workers in Zimbabwe. Inflation in Zimbabwe during 2006 is reported as being 1,281.11%, this developing at a time when GDP PPP was falling drastically[8]. In 2007 inflation was recorded at 66,212.3% whilst GDP PPP fell marginally[9]. This irrefutably proves than no economic theory is ever always right and one single observation can show us the limits to the models used to govern the economy. The output gap is a plausible method of visualizing inflationary projections within an economy but any single theory fails to account for black swan events such as excessive money printing as observed in Zimbabwe leading up to the currency's official abandonment in April 2009.

Currency only acts as a store of value if people believe that the currency will remain just that. Loss of confidence in a currency will increase the velocity of transactions and negate any conventional inflation model. One of the most prominent historic examples of a loss of faith in a currency's store of value was the German Deutschmark. Interestingly, when the money supply rapidly expanded in post WW1 Germany, it initially had a negligible effect on price inflation. I believe that Keynes's animal spirits plays a dominating role in explaining this. As economic conditions were deemed to be bleak - households were inclined to save rather than spend excess currency and so even as the money supply expanded; the velocity of transactions was not sufficient to create a rise in prices. This effect was short-lived, however, it illustrates that there can be a lag in inflation derived from a rapid expansion of money supply.

Investing in Oligopolistic Industries

In short, an oligopolistic market is said to exist if the five largest firms occupy more than fifty-percent of the industry. In the UK, oligopolies exist in the supermarket, banking and gambling sectors. Breaking into an oligopolistic market can be a very lucrative achievement for an outside enterprise. This was demonstrated by the German discount supermarket brands capturing market share in the UK supermarket sector. If investing in a company that is part of an oligopoly, this should be a prime consideration as elevated profits will entice competition.

Oligopolistic firms are likely to establish and reinforce existing barriers to entry in a bid to warn off potential competition from new entrants. This can take on many forms, economies of scale may be a key determinant owing to the size of the firms. Advertising expenditure can create barriers to entry, this is evident with bookmakers such as William Hill. Aggressive advertising regimes can taper smaller rival endeavors to compete for market share as advertising campaigns successfully corner the market and expose branding in a fashion that lower capitalized rivals cannot compete with. Providing barriers to entry are high, investing in companies that occupy an oligopoly can be extremely profitable as market share is relatively secure from new entrants. If barriers to entry are absent or low - the oligopoly will likely be transformed into a more fragmented market structure. If a market is contestable, that is, there is freedom to enter and exit then inducement to enter the market will be high for rival companies.

The structure of an oligopoly will vary with the level of competition between firms. In certain markets, price wars may be used to capture market share from rival firms. If investing in an oligopolistic company, the investor should pay close attention to the action of the other participating companies. Within an oligopoly, firms are interdependent - the actions of one firm will impact on rivals whose reactions will in turn affect their rivals.

One final note is markets where a larger and more dominant participant exists, their dominant share of the market can allow them to become an 'enforcer'. In the event of another enterprise reducing prices to gain market share, the enforcer could punish the firm by expanding output and simultaneously dropping prices. This activity will result in a reduction of profit for all companies engaged in the oligopoly and can act as a stark warning not to meddle with price cuts.

Similar occurrences of this sort of activity has occurred in the oil market in which the low cost producer Saudi Arabia has expanded output to harm rival producers for geopolitical motives. A dominant firm may be able to rely on funds accrued from previous sales to sustain a period of selling below cost in order to drive smaller rivals out of business, they may also have better access to external capital than rivals due to their track record. The chief consideration being that losses incurred whilst selling below costs must be eclipsed by the profits available when the firm rises costs after the insolvencies of rival companies.

3

PRIMARY COMMODITIES

What Affects the Price of Commodities?

In short, commodities are subject to market forces like any other asset. This being supply, demand and expectation. The real rate (adjusted for inflation) of interest can impact commodity prices. If the real rate is negative then capital will duly flow into assets such as commodities – as the opportunity cost of holding non-yield assets reduces. This gives rise to an inverse relationship between the strength of the US dollar and the price of commodities. Generally speaking, a rise in the dollar will invariably, ceteris paribus, cause a general fall in commodity prices.

More specifically, an expansion of economic growth has been an important causal factor of previous commodity booms. However, it is important to note that not all instances of marked economic growth give rise to a commodity price boom. Other factors will likely need to be present for substantial price rises, these being low inventories and tight production capacities. These preconditions are often present after prolonged periods of depressed prices.

In these circumstances, supply would be limited due to the absence of significant profit conjoined with low prices that act to reduce the need for high inventories. This gives some clarity and weight to the expression 'low prices are a cure for low prices'. The gravity of the price boom will, in some cases, prove to be commodity specific. This being due to the time lag in responding to a price rise. Supply capacity can be more nimble in agricultural commodities relative to metals or fuels. Years can pass from the discovery of an oil field to it becoming operational.

Furthermore, given the perishable nature of agricultural commodities, it is unfeasible to store crops for excessive periods which makes them susceptible to rapid price increases in the event of a short term supply crisis.

Commodity Producing Companies

High commodity prices and profits encourage organizational slack which can lead to inefficiencies. These high profits relax cost discipline – allowing the cost of production to rise. Conversely, depressed commodity prices and profits induce cost reduction practices.

Rising prices make it economical for high-cost projects such as deep water oil wells and underground mineral mines, whereas low prices will result in the moratorium of the highest cost ventures. This is an important consideration when investing in oil exploration/production companies that operate in deep offshore fields. If the commodity prices fall below the average cost of extraction, viability in production will be undermined.

Investing in stocks that produce primary commodities conveys added risk because not only is the company subject to the risks of enterprises from other sectors such as mismanagement, funding issues, director fraud, stock market crashes and influences of foreign government policies. They are also largely exposed to the additional risk of commodity price movements with their share prices often adhering to price movements of the underlying commodity. Furthermore, as production typically occurs in foreign countries - foreign exchange fluctuations create opportunities as well as risk for these corporations.

Given the example of a South African platinum producing company; platinum will be sold on the international market in US dollars (USD). Their inputs such as staff wages will be in South African Rand (ZAR). A fall in ZAR against the USD will result in the company's costs falling in conjunction with a rise in revenue. The obverse is valid too, an adverse movement of the exchange rate can result in costs rising relative to revenue. This convergence will have a significant impact on profitability of said company's share price. Identifying trends between a currency coupling will act as a signal to future earnings. This of course can be offset if the company engages in foreign exchange hedges, details on which will be found in the company annual reports.

The Substitution Effect

Price volatility can be particularly extreme in commodities with no close substitute. In a supply disruption of wheat, consumption can tend towards oats and lessen demand of wheat. If a material can perform a similar function to the commodity that is subject to a supply crisis; then consumption would gravitate to the good that is available providing it is not excessively priced – relatively speaking. This is of interest to the investor of mineral producing companies. For instance, in the event of a supply crisis of copper, silver harbors many of coppers desirable attributes yet due to the disparity between their prices, copper would need to appreciate substantially before it becomes economical to substitute it with silver.

Substitutes for individual commodities will often be found in the same group. Therefore, these commodities will tend to move in concert. For example precious metals such as Gold, Silver and Platinum generally move in tandem. This is an important consideration when ensuring diversification within a portfolio. Spreading one's purchases between Gold and Silver is not an effective form of diversification as they will respond similarly to any given fundamental development in the market. If an event causes Gold to depreciate then the price of Silver will duly follow suit.

Shifts in agricultural commodities tend to be caused by supply side disturbances such as adverse weather. Whereas, demand shocks are more likely to impact mineral prices. In the case of the precious metals, huge inventories of Gold exist around the world and can act as a shock absorber if there was a disruption of supply. A rise in price will likely be met with a supply of Gold to the market from existing inventories as holders look to cash their profits.

Platinum is more prone to supply shocks as the production of platinum is much more concentrated than that of Gold, with South Africa and Russia being large producing countries. Miner strikes in the past have caused supply issues which have influenced the price of commodities such as Platinum. This only really is observed in commodities that has geographic supply concentrations.

Price Floors and the Shutdown Rule

Given the costs involved in production of commodities, there is a price floor. If market prices fall below the cost of production, even the lowest cost producers in the market will eventually go bust. This causing a supply crisis after which prices can begin to rise and find a higher equilibrium. Implicit in this view, commodities such as Oil or Gold will never fall to zero, unlike some equities.

It is a common finding to observe companies from various sectors producing at a loss. Whether this be due to low commodity prices as recently seen with coal miners, or if a low-cost producer has entered the market and is causing disruption. This being previously seen in the solar panel industry when Chinese companies began dumping into the international market.

If a firm is knowingly selling its product/commodity at a loss, then why not cease operations? The answer can be found with the shutdown rule. Which, although seemingly paradoxical, states that it can be beneficial for the lossmaking firm to maintain a level of output rather that shutdown operations.

The shutdown rule is best explained by distinguishing between the various costs incurred by a firm. A company will have fixed liabilities such as licensing costs of a mine, security guard contracts, debt interest and/or rent of a factory. They will also have average variable costs such as fuel inputs to run machinery and staff wages. These costs vary with the level of output, by shutting down operations the firm can abolish most of these variable costs altogether – machinery that sits idle burns no fuel and staff can be retired from duty. If the loss making firm can generate enough revenue to cover its fixed costs then it should maintain output even if it is making an overall loss. If the company finds that it is not generating enough revenue to cover all of its operational expenses but can cover its fixed costs - then it would be beneficial to maintain output. If the enterprise ceased operations altogether, it would still have to pay its fixed liabilities leading to an even bigger loss.

In the above example, a coal miner paying $100,000 per month to operate a mine will still need to meet that obligation whether they are selling the coal from the mine or not. It's better to produce at a loss and pay the £100,000 through sales of mined coal than to sit idle and burn cash reserves.

A loss-making firm must consider its position in such a circumstance because there are costs involved in shutting down during periods of low commodity prices and then reopening when conditions are more favorable. Some mining companies may prefer to keep unprofitable mines operating by subsidizing them from more profitable ones, rather than closing them. This will invariably lead to a philosophy of maximizing production despite high costs, in turn exacerbating losses when prices are depressed for long periods.

Dutch Disease & the Resource Trap

It is conceivable that a significant discovery of a natural resource could be a shortcut to prosperity and enable economies with low GDP per capita to leapfrog other more established economies. History repeatedly shows that this is often not the case and in some instances a backwards economy benefits, on aggregate, very little from a world class natural resource discovery.

Commodity exports cause the incumbent country's currency to rise relative to other currencies. In turn this makes the country's other export activities less competitive. In essence, natural resource exports crowd out manufacturing by keeping the currency strong.

Profits from the booming commodity producing sector cause an increase in demand for products from the other sectors. The price for these goods are determined outside of the country, companies cannot sell their goods for more than the international price as otherwise it will substitute demand in favor of cheaper imports from lower priced foreign companies. Increases in domestic demand will be satisfied by imports which will retard growth in these domestic sectors.

The situation for the goods and services sectors deteriorate as the booming commodity sector attracts labor and pushes domestic wages higher. There is facility for human capital to flow out of other sectors into commodity producing companies that are offering higher wages. The increase in profits from the commodity sector allow for absorption of the increase in labor costs. The same cannot be said for the other goods and services sectors that did not experience an increase in profits and so their international competitiveness is lost.

Under normal circumstances, a loss of competitiveness would lead to current account deterioration which would encourage an exchange rate devaluation. In turn, restoring some competitiveness to the goods and services sector. A booming commodity sector ensures growth in the export sector and prevents the current account degradation that would be required for an exchange rate revaluation. A situation emerges in which the currencies exchange rate begins to intertwine with the price of the commodity. In short, the strong growth of commodity export activities ensures that the domestic currency is maintained at a level that makes other sectors uncompetitive, raising the propensity in imports from other economies.

Nigeria in the 1970s experienced such a situation in which the revenues from oil sales made other exports such as cocoa uncompetitive with the production of the latter collapsing. Dutch disease can taper growth by crowding out export activities that would prosper under normal conditions. During a boom phase, there can be an overreliance on revenue from commodity exports, this can lead to devastating consequences should the market price of that commodity crash. This was recently evident with Venezuela when the price of oil collapsed. In these situations foreign aid is rendered relatively impotent, the resource endowed countries have capital going to its government but is often not put to good use. Empirical observation has taught us that there is one exception to this consensus in which aid can facilitate development, this being when the country is in a process of reform and incipient turnaround.

Other Sources of Dutch Disease

Dutch disease is not confined to economies with a large commodity exporting sector. Critics have argued that the recipients of foreign aid are also subject to weak growth due to the retardation of exports. By receiving vast amounts of foreign capital, the exchange rate appreciates and erodes away at some of any existing competitive advantage that may have existed in low cost producing countries. This should not be too much of an issue if the capital is used to stimulate productivity but if the capital is squandered then it compounds the problem.

Economists have pointed to economies like the United Kingdom (UK) having an overvalued currency due to the unrivalled financial hub of London. The provision of financial services has arguably led to a crowding out of other sectors of the economy. This implies that any weakening of the financial services sector will likely aid the UK's manufacturing and other general export sectors.

The Eurozone and the Euro currency has been subject to criticism for conditions that are created that mimic the Dutch disease. The currency union was arguably based upon the US Dollar model - that could promote trade due to removing barriers that different floating currencies bring. The reality is that the currency union has created a scenario in which winners and losers have developed. Germany is arguably the main beneficiary as a strong German export sector would usually cause a rise of the German currency to appreciate to a level that would render exports uncompetitive. This has not been the case as many of the unproductive peripheral European economies have acted as a deadweight on the currency's exchange. Pockets of high unemployment in countries such as Spain and Greece have weighed down on the value of the Euro. Under normal circumstances, countries with high unemployment would lead to a reduction in aggregate demand and the currency would devalue causing a stimulating effect on the exporting sector. Failing this, the central banks may choose to embark of policies that cause a depreciation of the exchange rate.

With a single currency across the bloc, the countries that would otherwise have benefitted from a devaluing currency have been stuck with a currency that is being supported by strong exporting countries such as Germany and France. The Euro is acting like a fiscal straightjacket for the weaker European countries in a similar fashion to how a Gold standard would restrict actions of the central bank.

So why does the US not have states with high unemployment? The answer lies in the freedom of the workforce. If unemployment in a state increases, workers are free to move to adjacent states where demand is higher causing a mobility of labor. This is not as easily done in the Eurozone due to language barriers. A Greek student may be unable to relocate to countries with higher demand for workers such as Germany because he does not speak German. This is even more pronounced if a family has monolingual young children receiving education in their domicile country.

Hence, a by-product of the single currency across a wide demographic can be pockets of high unemployment in less productive economies caused by factors that reduce the propensity for depreciation of the exchange rate, much like Dutch Disease.

Agriculture

One of the best pieces of advice given to me is to look for investments where prices are depressed and positive changes are occurring. These markets will typically evade the interest of the media and retail investors. Finding opportunities like this is often easier said than done. However, I believe that there is such a situation is emerging in the agricultural market. Generally, markets that are being ignored hold the best value and agriculture rarely is mentioned in market reports.

Engle's Law claims that as income rises - the proportion spent on food decreases. This is important for countries with low GDP per capita in which a large proportion of income is spent on basic necessities. For instance, USDA/Economic research service in 2008 published their findings that as a percentage of income the Kenyan and Pakistan population spent 44.9% and 45.4% of their income on food. Whereas, the USA and United Kingdom spent 6.8% and 8.9% respectively[10]. If some of the World's poorest countries begin to converge with more prosperous economies - current consumption trends will be transformed which will cause a huge shift in demand.

As a general concept, if on aggregate, people's incomes rise they will demand more of most goods even if the price remains unchanged. A distinction between classifications of goods will help to explain the extent of the opportunity over the next generation with investment in agriculture.

Goods can be classified as:

Inferior goods – As incomes rise, fewer of these are demanded as incomes are increased

Normal goods – As incomes rise the amount of normal goods will increase proportionately

Luxury (Veblen) goods – Demand for luxury goods increases more that any given proportionate rise in income.

The World Bank in 2011 reported that the global demand for grain has stagnated whilst demand for meat is rising faster than the population[11]. In poverty stricken countries, there is a natural tendency to consume inferior goods which translates into a basic diet. As incomes rise, there should be a tendency to transition away from basic grain diets to the increase in consumption of meat. In short, food inferior goods will be replaced with normal goods such as meat.

With more arable farmers switching to livestock one can see how the grain markets could be more susceptible than ever to a supply crisis. To add weight to this argument, the current median age of farmers in the UK is 59 years old[12]. Most independent studies report that the occupation with the highest suicide rate is farming, possibly due to the hardship of the business and the ease of access to chemicals or devices that could easily end one's life.

Many UK farmers in the midlands have excavated their arable land to convert them into fishing lakes which tends to have much less maintenance and a higher associated yield. These findings further imply that the supply side of agriculture is potentially heading for a crisis. An exacerbating factor being that agricultural goods are perishable, therefore there may be an absence of inventories to offset the reduction in supply capacity. This should not be ignored by the investor, opportunities to capitalize will be purchasing agricultural commodity future contracts, fertilizing and tractor supply companies as well as businesses that produce agricultural commodities, particularly meat farmers.

Developments in China will influence the agricultural markets. China accounts for approximately twenty percent of the world's population whilst providing only seven percent of the world's arable land[13]. China previously adopted a large scale drive to increase food production after the 'great famine' of 1960. Since then, China has conceded millions of acres of farmland to industrial sites following the success of its economic expansion. Given the rise in living standard in China, importing food is now more prevalent than years of past. For example, with its rising affluence China is an important customer for crab exporters on the Southern Coast of Cornwall England. At least it was until an embargo was placed on the UK crabs due to an alleged concentration of metallic concentrate within the crab meat.

4

EMERGING ECONOMIES

Emerging economies have been a significant focal point of many commentator's reviews within the investment community. The allure of these markets being the potential for sustained exponential growth. Whilst development may be exceptional in these economies, it is often extraordinarily volatile with regular crises. One very important consideration for any investor to recognize that just because emerging markets have the potential to converge with the western economies - it does not mean that they will.

A reported eighty percent of the world's population resides in emerging economies and so there is a catastrophic enticement for western multinational companies to tap into these markets[14]. What should not be overlooked is the emerging market domestic companies are fending off multinational competition for market share. There is many advantages to fighting on your own turf – they may have a greater cultural understanding, more appropriate business models and may have contacts in government.

History has shown the ease in which rapidly expanding emerging economies have stagnated once the easy gains of economic catch-up have been exhausted. A large source of this being imitation of their more developed counterparts in western countries. Where established economies need to invest in R&D to discover new innovative technologies and techniques, poorer countries can simple imitate their richer neighbor's ideas at a fraction of the cost. A prime example of this was in the pharmaceutical industry in which there was a momentous paradigm of Indian pharmaceutical firms producing generic versions of on-patent drugs. By reverse engineering - the Indian companies could determine how to produce the molecule that may have taken a large foreign multinational company millions of dollars and years' worth of investment to produce.

Infant Industry Tariffs

In poor and inefficient economies, tariffs can be implemented to sow the seeds of economic growth. If a firm in any given industry has a 'learning curve', that is, when they expand output they can reduce marginal costs by 'learning-by-doing' – then when a company initially starts production it will undoubtedly have costs higher than that of mature overseas rivals. This has been found to be particularly frequent in the manufacturing sector. Thus, when domestic firms experience higher costs than international rivals - competition from imports will replace demand from budding firms and they will be unable to sell their produce. A responsible government would therefore allow temporary tariffs which will impose a tax on imports and allow their incumbent firms or industries to learn and develop. What would not be sound economic policy is to grant domestic firms permanent protection and allow inefficient firms protection form lower cost imports. This will encourage slack and be detrimental to consumers. Allowing natural competition is healthy as it encourages innovation and efficiency.

The Race to the Bottom

The phase 'race to the bottom' is often used in discussion centralized on emerging economies. The term is a shorthand description for the result of competitive forces causing pressure on firms to produce as cheaply as possible. Prices will tend to drop to just above the lowest aggregate cost, this being coined as 'the bottom'. Any producers that fail to function at these prices will be forced out of the market – leaving the lowest cost producers to supply demand for goods.

The race to the bottom is a derivative of open market policies which act to enhance purchasing power parity within the economy as the country's firms are better positioned to compete internationally. If a parallel economy chose instead to implement a protectionist strategy, costs would be free to rise as inefficient firms would have protection from more productive foreign rivals. Further, collusion between domestic firms could push prices even higher at the customer's cost. This sort of activity would be nullified if barriers to trade were removed.

The Poverty Trap

A poverty trap is said to develop when poverty has effects acting as causes of poverty. A country in a poverty trap may have a series of vicious cycles, processes of circular and cumulative causation in which traits of poverty reinforce themselves.

For instance, a function of poverty is poor nutrition. This can lead to lowered productivity causing insufficient wages within an economy's work force, thus preventing economic development. Malaria keeps countries poor because a disease prevalence increases poverty as it impacts the workforce by reducing human capital. Workers are prevented from becoming more experienced and efficient as they are struck with fatal diseases. Furthermore children are withdrawn from formal education as they become ill from tropical diseases. As poverty trapped countries are poor, the potential market for a vaccine fails to entice the research and development investments that multinational pharmaceutical companies would require to justify the allocation of required investment.

Further vicious circles exist in the poverty trap, a low level of manufacturing leads to poor infrastructure and limited technical ability as workers do not develop from learning-by-doing activities. The poor infrastructure hampers any competitiveness in manufacturing as the cost of producing and transporting goods is high. Poor economic activity prevents social programs such as world class healthcare or educational systems; the absence of these can act as a hindrance on future economic growth and so it is simple to see how many countries that are poor, stay poor.

Geography – the Landlocked Problem

Something that the mainstream economics books will not teach you is the impact that geography can have on the prosperity of a country. Past literature has found that being 'landlocked', that is, a country that shares borders with other countries instead of a coastline; can reduce growth by half a percentage point[15]. Of course, this rule has exceptions such as Switzerland and Austria which have high growth rates but there is a reasoning behind this. Generally speaking, the applicability of the landlocked problem is most prominent in Africa. The problem stems from the fact that transport costs for a landlocked country is contingent on the transport infrastructure of its coastal neighbors. As aforementioned, Switzerland is a landlocked country but it is adjacent to advanced countries with excellent transport links.

If a country is landlocked and its neighbors have poor transport links to the coast this will be out of its control. This will make it difficult to engage in international trade, especially exporting goods with a high transport costs such as those products of the manufacturing sector. One exception to the landlocked problem being a country that is endowed with natural resources as these commodities are often so valuable that it is still economical to export them even with the higher cost of transport. Therefore, if there is significant infrastructure investment in a coastal country; it may make its landlocked neighbors more competitive in the export market and lead to increased growth. For obvious reasons this situation can be considered as an early indicator that economic prospects could start to improve for the landlocked country.

It is not unusual for coastal countries to focus on supplying the international markets, landlocked countries however may be rendered uncompetitive by exogenous factors as mentioned. Often, then, these markets will shift focus on supplying their domestic or adjacent markets with goods and services. The issue arises when the landlocked country is producing the same goods as its neighbor. In lieu of complimenting one another and growing in harmony - they will instead be competing for market share. The optimal strategy is to attempt to supply their neighboring markets with goods and services that it is not already producing itself - preferably exercising any comparative advantage the landlocked economy has.

It is not unusual for the prosperity of landlocked countries to be inextricably linked with that of their neighbors, this effectively acting as a spillover of either wealth or poverty. This has been observed in Africa, the difference with this continent is there is very little wealth to spill over. It is paramount for a landlocked country to adopt good economic and political policies to prohibit their human capital deserting the country in favor of a more prosperous or desirable neighbor. An additional consideration is given the interconnectedness of landlocked and neighboring countries is the landlocked country will be susceptible to any bad policy decisions made by adjacent economy governments.

One of the self-reinforcing aspects of the landlocked trap is that as prospects of landlocked countries can be severely handicapped. There can be a paradigm for the economy to hemorrhage its human capital in favor of better prospects. In some cases in the past, landlocked countries have been annexed by their neighbors to form a conjoined country as there was little incentive for the weaker country to stay an independent entity. An obvious example of a national concatenation being the reunification of East and West Germany to form the single country that it is today.

The Demographic Dividend

Analysts that seek opportunities in backward economies offering the best potential for growth will not only need to avoid investing in prospects that transpire to be only attractive 'on paper' - but they must also need to optimize the timing of the investment to avoid decadal inactivity. Backwards economies can stagnate for years prior to any marked acceleration of economic growth. There is a risk of making an excellent investment decision but not in the expected timescale. Additionally, there have been many examples of poor economies that have looked well placed for growth which never materialized. A leading indicator to a country's potential for a rapid rise in income being the demographic dividend, this can be used to identify an early catalyst for growth - offering some guidance on a timeframe for entry.

The notion of the demographic dividend applies to the transition of the structure of an economy's age distribution, which provides a positive shock to the economy. Traditionally, many economists and policy makers would assume that an increase in birth-rate would be good for economic growth. After all, countries prosper if their workforce is large relative to other groups in society that depend on the product of the labor force such as the young or the elderly. Children are future workers and so will reduce the median age of the population. However, many countries in Africa show us that there is much more to economic development than a youthful population. For instance, Zimbabwe has a reported population median age of 20.6 years of age[16]. Examples of situations in which demographic changes that have facilitated a country's growth being predominantly a decline in the population's birth and death rates as detailed below.

One of the vital requisites for this demographic gift to unfold is a fall in both mortality and fertility rates. The immediate reduction in birthing rates will allow for the reallocation of resources for investment in economic development and family welfare. Here, less capital is expended to satisfy the demands of infants which act as dead weights on the labor force. Large numbers of dependent children lead to more mothers having limited interaction with the labor market, thus precluding them from developing their human capital. Once a demographic dividend is capitalized on, it is a transient stimulus which presents as only a temporary window of opportunity. It is noteworthy that if a situation occurs in which the distribution of age within an economy is becoming favorable for economic growth does not necessarily mean that any expected benefit is a foregone conclusion. Economies may satisfy the preconditions to receive a demographic dividend, yet fail to experience favorable growth.

The release of resources from a fall in fertility will need to be managed appropriately. The absence of policies that support growth due to these demographic changes will need to be in place or the risk of internal tensions will materialize due to a large pool of the unemployed workers. Empirical study shows us that countries that are experiencing a youth-bulge are more prone to political tensions. The consensus of literature on compatible policies all place significant weight on reducing unwanted pregnancies with the provision of contraceptives. In sum, opportunities derived from the demographic dividend are temporary and generally not repeated. The effects of the dividend are exacerbated by desirable policies in place that embrace education and job creation.

The Importance of Foreign Direct Investment (FDI) in Under Developed Countries

Many underdeveloped countries are shackled by a low equilibrium trap which is another self-reinforcing cycle. Here, the population's income per capita is of a level that is only consistent with fulfilling basic subsistence requirements. The population is too poor to save income for future investments and growth opportunities. In essence, new investments can only be fostered by the capital created from saving activities, if nothing is being saved - ceteris paribus - nothing is being invested. In the event that per capita income increases due to a technology advancement or resource discovery, it is said that population growth will also increase at a relative rate. In essence, households will respond to the receipt of an increase in wealth by having more children, aggregately speaking. The trap can be modelled by demonstrating income and demographic curves, points of inceptions will be equilibrium points for the economy.

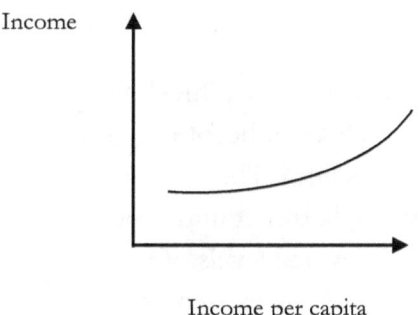

Income per capita

The above income curve model intimates that as GDP increases, GDP per capita should also increase. This holds as higher levels of GDP can entice further growth factors such as savings with associated reinvestment, FDI and development in human capital.

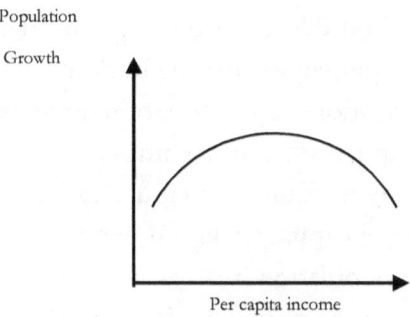

Per capita income

The demographic transitions model illustrates that families will respond to an increase in living standards by having more offspring until a threshold is breached. Hereafter, children become an economic burden and fertility declines. The main justification for the inverted parabola is that until reaching a certain threshold of elevated levels of income - couples will respond to an increased living standard by having more children. Deaths due to malnutrition and basic healthcare requirements will begin to taper. Consequently, population growth will be interconnected with any increase in aggregate income until a certain threshold is breached.

Thereafter, subsequent increases in income is met with a reduction in fertility rates as having a large number of children becomes an economic burden. This couples with the fact that once a higher income supports a reduction in lower mortality rates it becomes more difficult to reduce them further. The increase in population dilutes earnings per head and so there is a fall in per capita income back to subsistence level as more resources are required to sustain a larger population and the amount of resources is often constrained. Even if GDP is increasing, when the capital trickles down to an increased general population it is spread more sparingly and so per capita income is reduced.

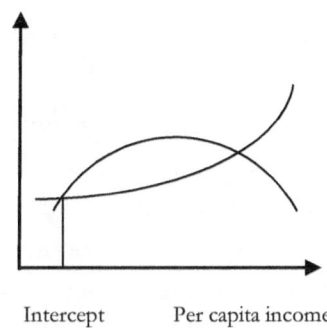

Income/population growth

Intercept   Per capita income

Evident in the low income equilibrium trap - the economy resides at the interception point. Any interception between the income and demographic curve reveal points in which the economy is in equilibrium. If one presupposes that the economy is residing at this interception - income and demographic growth are relatively subdued.

Any increase in FDI or adoption of a technology will cause growth in per capita income. The economy begins to transition up the income curve, however, the incidence of more income has an expansionary effect on the birthrate and so the economy also moves along the demographic curve. Given that population growth exceeds grown in per capita incomes, the income per capita will fall until it reaches its old equilibrium. This, being the low equilibrium trap.

For an economy that is stuck in a low equilibrium level trap, there are endeavors that will see the economy break out. Chiefly these will be emphasis on thrift and consequential investment. Policies limiting family size either through policies or investment in family planning with further expedite the per capita growth. Otherwise the only real plausible catalyst is to procure funding from foreign investment. This will fill the void left by domestic investment absence and in many situations is essential for lower developed economies to break out of their respective low income equilibrium traps.

Autocratic Economies

Other than Dutch disease, there is subsequent apt explanations as to why many of the small countries with world class natural resource reserves have populations living in abstract poverty. There is a suspicious correlation between populous living below poverty thresholds and autocratic governance. The devil in me wants to suggest that the absence of educational and social provisions is deliberate as an uneducated and low skilled population is easier to contain, exploit and control. If the average citizen lacks basic human capital they will meet more resistance when attempting to emigrate which further compounds the issue. Take, for instance, Jose Eduardo dos Santos of Angola. His net worth is estimated to be in the region of USD20 Billion[17]. Yet figures published by the World Bank reveal that Angola has a GDP Per capita of USD4,101[18]. The same source shows that Zimbabwe has a GDP per capita of USD924 whilst Robert Mugabe is said to have a net worth of c.USD10 million[19]. There is an incentive for these rich autocrats to endorse policies that protect their own interests.

Rich Countries with Poor People

Arguably one of the greatest paradoxes in the world economy is how states that export copious quantities of oil can have populations living in abstract poverty. The Dutch Disease helps explain part of this story but the root cause is embedded much deeper into the composition of the country's governance.

In a traditional balanced democratic economy, there exists a need for tax compliance. The incumbent tax systems allow for the government to operate and society to live harmoniously. However, if you are Kuwait or Venezuela the revenues from oil exports reduces the government's dependence on procuring taxes from its workforce. This is an extremely unpalatable situation to be in because tax reliance is coupled with accountability. If you are in a position where you do not need your workers to pay tax then who cares about the people? With less accountability, corruption becomes rife as the government loses its incentive to adhere to the needs of the people. The rentier state theory suggests that countries dependent on external rents such as commodity exports share a different relationship with their citizens than a similar diversified economy, in turn, reducing the likelihood of the state developing into a democracy.

There is further dependence on the commodity related sector as integration is perpetuated with the labor force becoming interconnected to the commodity exporting sector. The failure of an incentive to diversify their skills solidifies the economy's reliance on the commodity. Moreover, a further stratification unfolds as those that manage to acquire positions within the commodity producing industry are duly awarded whilst the rest are left behind.

Once an economy reaches this stage its fate is contingent on the price of the commodity. During periods of high prices, revenues are often squandered on wasteful projects like palaces for the privileged. Excessive profits being a platform for a surge in inequality. During periods of suppressed prices fiscal budgets deteriorate, the government begin to borrow from abroad often levied against natural resource reserves with debt escalating quickly. As a result of conditions borne from the effects of the Dutch Disease - many economies become net importers of food, exacerbating the ill effects on the general population when resource prices are low. It should not come as a surprise then that oil-dependent states are often more militaristic with large security forces; presumably as it is aligned to the interest of the powerful and hampers any attempt at a coup to capture precious oil fields.

5

CAPITAL FLOWS AND FOREIGN EXCHANGE

The very comprehension of capital flows movements can lead to excellent investment decisions and offer clues of when to enter a market. The cyclical paradigms of liquidity funneling can mean that in one sector of the economy such as the housing market you can have an inflationary effect yet in another sector there can be deflation – such as certain goods becoming cheaper. So both inflation and deflation can coexist and this is often determined, inter alia, by the behavior of capital flows.

A recurring phenomenon in the global markets is the capital flow bonanza. The incidence of bonanzas has increased as restrictions on international capital flows have been more relaxed globally. The paradigm often initiates with foreign investors perusing a developing country. Capital flows into small local financial markets causing the exchange rate to appreciate, asset prices boom and local commodity prices go ballistic. These favorable domestic asset prices improve the national fiscal indicators and allow for the expansion of domiciliary credit.

As a result of the rapid appreciation of the domestic currency, local authorities embark in large scale foreign exchange sales of local currency to temper the effects on the exchange rate, thus large accumulations of reserves are required to stabilize the exchange rate.

The marked inflow of capital can protract for some time, often lulling policymakers and investors alike to believe that the bonanza is a permanent phenomenon. When investors are bullish on the prospects of a market subject to a bonanza - they usually provide too much capital and therefore ignite a spending boom and an investment mania. This being prodromal for an inevitable downturn as excess capacity develops due to new market participants entering the booming sector.

Bonanzas typically preclude with an abrupt stop and subsequent reversal of capital flows. There is an association between bonanza periods and frequency of currency, banking and inflation shocks. Capital flow bonanzas systematically precede sovereign defaults. Real GDP growth tends to accelerate in the period immediately preceding a bonanza and then falls thereafter. Equity prices increase when capital flows in and retreat when capital reverses course, this being emblematic of a complete boom and bust cycle.

Sudden stops usually occur when capital no longer flows into an emerging economy, leaving it unable to maintain an excess of consumption over income. Empirical literature on this subject suggests that consensus is that capital flow bonanzas can last for between two and four years[20]. This being why many market participants believe the bonanza to be permanent. On some occasions, bonanzas can be separated by periods in excess of a year which can draw out the episode and lead to the false assumption that it is permanent rather than transitory.

Observation has showed us that the three leading catalysts to a bonanza is reductions in international interest rates, economic growth in advanced economies and a large-scale commodity price boom. When growth stagnates in advanced economies, capital searches for yield and profit opportunities in emerging economies. Therefore, notwithstanding the positive effects of higher export revenues from favorable commodity profits, an underlying impetus for global commodity prices is low or negative real interest rates.

Global Liquidity

With excessive global liquidity sloshing around the world economy, this pool of capital will flow to boost some economic activity causing an appreciation of an asset market somewhere in the world. Policies that favor the loosening of liquidity will duly allow asset bubbles to inflate but seldom are able to determine which market(s) with receive the gush of capital flows. One of the most important points to realize in respect to capital flows is that when the investment community is engaged with a fashionable investment theme; outstanding opportunities will invariably be found elsewhere. A large-scale bull market in an asset class will suck capital out of other markets which will cause them to become depressed. Under these conditions, they offer a very attractive risk versus reward valuation. In fact, the greater the mania in one sector of an economy the more likely that there will be other markets offering excellent buying opportunities.

A strong US dollar and stock market will eventually peter out - once investors decide to reallocate their capital one must inspect where this capital will likely flow. It is this that allows the investor to position himself accordingly whilst others are still distracted by the overheating asset market. Whilst recessions can offer attractive asset price valuations, investment manias derived from capital flow bonanzas can offer once in a lifetime selling opportunities.

Many market participants comment on the printing of currency practices that the central banks are currently committing to. The obvious hedge against cash depreciation being to hold physical Gold. Whilst this is a plausible strategy, it should not be overlooked that Gold is a high-risk investment because of the absence of cashflow. This is not to say that Gold cannot be an excellent investment under anything but unfavorable conditions.

In a money printing environment, markets will appreciate but not all at once and not all at the same magnitude. Some of this excess liquidity will flow into stocks, housing and commodities. There are circumstances where the conditions that allow capital flows are distorted by the act of pegging currencies. This will duly act as an exacerbating factor or hindrance on cross border capital movements.

Currency pegs

A currency peg is a scenario in which a government decides on a specific level of exchange rate. Locked exchange rates are desirable for policy makers because they can reduce uncertainty for trade between two or more countries. It may also increase the allure for foreign investors as they will believe the home currency will be stable. The problem with fixing two currencies is events can unfix them. For a government to maintain this fixed rate, it must commit its central bank to make any necessary currency transactions to maintain the exchange rate. Fixing a home currency against another country's currency is often performed without consulting the other country's government. Currency pegs have made speculators fortunes in the past. If investors develop an intuition that the country that is fixing its currency to the 'anchor currency' will not be able to sustain the rate, they will position themselves accordingly. When pegs break it usually does so with force as markets often overreact to sudden events by overshooting in either direction.

The fixed exchange rate, therefore, warrants inclusion in any literature centralized on investment economics. Monitoring the developments between two economies that are subject to a fixed exchange rate can yield clues that market forces may eventually cause the peg to break. A necessity of adopting a fixed exchange rate is effectively surrendering the home country's right to manage its own monetary policies to influence domestic aggregate demand. Given that a tinkering of the interest rate will adjust capital flow, if one of the featured countries commits to an interest rate reduction to stimulate aggregate demand - it would increase the propensity for foreign investors to withdraw their capital - placing downward pressure on the exchange rate. The foreign policy makers would have to interpose to offset this capital flight by imitating the reduction in interest rates or risk abandoning the peg completely.

The UK government opted to join an Exchange rate mechanism (ERM) by fixing the pound against the German Deutsche mark (DM) in 1990. It was believed that this action would stabilize inflation and allow the UK to experience German prosperity and growth. The pound was fixed without negotiation, many analysts suggested that the pound was fixed too high, in turn, overvaluing the pound. This being 1GBP / 2.95DM.

Immediately after the pound joined the ERM unemployment rates began to ascend as businesses struggled to sell their goods abroad. For the first time in post-war history, families were selling their houses for less than was paid. In 1992 the Bundes Bank council raised interest rates in a bid to extinguish domestic price increases. In theory, the Bank of England would have to match the interest rate changes to maintain the pound's value against the DM. However, it was deemed that this would cause too much disruption in the housing market and harm an already faltering economy. Investment banks began to sell pounds and buy DMs because of the high German interest rates - pushing the pound to its bottom limit inside the ERM. The UK government attempted to reassure the market, subsequent interest rate rises was agreed and implemented but was not enough to offset speculators selling the pound.

The bank of England had a reported £19billion in foreign currency holdings. At the height of the crisis in 1997, the bank of England was losing £2billion per hour in transactions to maintain the exchange rate[21]. Rates were raised to 15% in desperation. Eventually the government suspended supportive measures and the pound crashed out of the ERM with sellers of the pound making significant profits.

As the above example illustrates, whilst participating in a currency peg the base interest rate acts as a mechanism for managing the exchange rate rather than aggregate demand within the economy, thus the participating country accepts the monetary policy of the anchor country. Herein lies the problem as divergences in the fundamentals within the two economies places strain on maintaining the exchange rate. In this instance, a government can decide to alter the level at which the two currencies are fixed, otherwise market forces will cause a significant movement as the peg breaks and currencies disperse. The abandonment of a peg will result in the weaker economy devaluing its currency, which in turn, will offset the trade deficit. On occasion, an economy may opt for a revaluation in which the exchange rate is increased to strengthen the home currency which corrects a trade surplus. Similar situations to currency pegs occur when countries abandon their own currency and replace it with another. This situation developed in Zimbabwe after the hyperinflation where the country reverted to the US Dollar in order to trade. The Indian Rupee and South African Rand was also instated. Should these currencies appreciate in value it will starve off any threat of inflation but may lead to inefficient Zimbabwean companies struggling to compete in the international market. These conditions mean that Zimbabwe's economic output is contingent upon the actions of foreign policy makers in setting the price of their respective currencies via interest rates and the likes.

Fiscal Stimulus & Cross Border Money Flows

A severe limitation faced by central banks is that they can influence the amount of liquidity flowing around an economy but they cannot control where the capital flows are directed. An explanation to the lack of effectiveness in Quantitative Easing (QE) programs is that the fiscal and monetary stimulus may be occurring in the west but much of the production is actually occurring in the East. Therefore, policies engineered to stimulate the American and European economies is actually causing a rise in productivity in places such as Asia. With this comes a rise in prices, wages and living standards in the eastern economies through central bank activism in the west.

In short, the west consumes and the east produces. Globalization has attenuated the potency of fiscal policies because of capital flows across borders and tends to favor the lower cost producers. If you view QE in Japan and the US in terms of how well it has caused equities to appreciate then it has been a huge success. If, however, you measured it in terms of how it has effected the real economy then it has made little difference. These examples have demonstrated to us that printing currency can lift equities whereas at the same time the real economy can continue to decline.

Furthermore, if the European Central Bank engages in QE it may have the desired effect to increase economic output at some level, however, there is justification that much of this liquidity will flow into different markets and boost asset price inflation elsewhere. In the absence of capital border prohibition - one should always expect that a large scale increase in central bank activism will likely cause capital to leak out of said domestic areas and cause a boost in demand in more favorable markets as this liquidity pool chases yield elsewhere. If money is printed in the US it does not necessarily have to stimulate the US economy or create domestic inflation. It can stimulate any economy and cause inflation within other countries.

Foreign Exchange & Enterprise Risk

Fluctuations in the exchange rate has a ripple effect throughout the economy. Simply put, some enterprises will benefit and some will not. Structural FX risks are one of the more sinister currency risks that multinational firms are exposed to. In short, structural risks are borne from situations in which a company's cash outflows and inflows are impacted by fluctuations in the exchange rate. A European enterprise that exports to the US market is subject to structural risk as it obtains sales in US Dollars yet incurs costs in euros. Should the price of the euro appreciate against the dollar it will erode profit margins. For this reason a strong domestic currency encourages and necessitates entrepreneurs to become more efficient to compete internationally.

Price inflation could align prices over the longer term, however, such deviations in purchasing power often are reduced by fifty percent, on average, over two to three years. What complicates matters is often products are priced by global competition. For instance, the European corporation exporting goods to the US will have less exposure to the UD Dollar if all of its rival companies selling in the US market are also producing in the Eurozone. Clarity is further distorted on this matter if other rival companies are producing in the UK and have their production costs in Pounds Sterling. This will lead the European enterprise exposed to not only the US Dollar, but also the British Pound. This is because a fall in British Pound will allow for the UK producers to underprice their European rivals based on nominal exchange rate fluctuations.

A solution to managing this vulnerability to the US Dollar is by means of 'natural hedging'. By moving some of their production to the USA, the company will have an increased share of their operational costs in US Dollars which is immune to exchange rate movements. This strategy is very efficient in situations whereby a large proportion of sales occur in the country in question. This strategy losses potency if the associated cost of moving production is high which places competitive advantages at risk. Furthermore, this strategy is not applicable if it conflicts with the branding of the company. A Swiss chocolate maker may lose its identity if it produces products out of a factory in Texas.

A further FX risk to consider is transactional risk whereby there is a oscillation in FX movement in the interval between when a sale is unconditionally agreed and when the funds are actually outlaid. It is customary for companies to agree a 90 days settlement in Europe. The drawback from this sort of transition risk is that it will not benefit from an adjustment in purchasing power parity as even if prices did converge to offset the exchange movement, the two parties have already agreed terms of the deal.

Owing to the relatively short term nature of these settlements, they rarely cause companies financial distress and are easy to manage via hedging with financial instruments. Rolls Royce reported in 2016 that it had incurred an on-paper £2billion write down on its currency hedge book after the results of the EU referendum caused the pound to crash against the US Dollar[22]. This highlights the importance of distinguishing between a company that exercises responsible FX hedging and one that has a bolt on casino in the name of currency speculation using shareholder funds.

Investing in Precious Metals

Irrespective of current or future investment themes, I believe that an investor should always have some exposure to precious metals. A passage was therefore warranted in a book that concerns itself with investment risk and economics. The precious metals is a putative hedge against loss of purchasing power of currencies. As a currency depreciates, its purchasing power begins to erode. This translates into more pounds being required to purchase the same item(s). In terms of Gold - this creates the illusion that Gold is appreciating in price against the respective currency but in reality - the currency has lost some of its relative value and so it takes more of these depreciated pounds to buy the same ounce of

Gold. There are several merits to any portfolio containing precious metals and so the true dilemma is a question of the scale of the position.

The metals do not have a cashflow and so the returns of this investment class is defined by market valuations. In the UK, platinum and silver is subject to 20% value added tax but Gold is free from this surcharge. The metals have no interest yield, there is no dividend or coupon and so these assets convey an associated opportunity cost. Capital that is allocated for purchases of bigots or coins could be invested elsewhere and receive a cashflow. The magnitude of the opportunity cost is contingent on the real interest rates and dividend yields of other investments.

Often investors obsess over the allure of investing in Gold because of central bank intervention diluting the currency supply by printing fiat currency. I would like to add that mining activities are ever increasing the supply of Gold into the market in a similar fashion; the difference being the government can print pound notes but it cannot print Gold. In recent times much of this Gold has been purchased directly from the mines by the respective domicile governments – China being a prime example. I prefer holding physical gold to gold mining companies. If you want to make big money then you should be in exploration companies but at the same time out of a hundred companies if two will make it that's about the maximum. It's very difficult to make money in mining, the costs of exploration, appraising and extraction have risen very substantially in recent years and the interposing of foreign governments that demand increases in their interests of the resource source is unfavorable to the commodity producing industry.

Like most other sectors, during a financial crisis mining companies will encounter problems in financing exploration and exploitation of proven resources as these activities are typically very capital intensive. The survivorship bias also plays its part in skewing the perceptions of mining company success. It is very easy to consider the small mining companies that were transformed by world class discoveries but neglect to consider the amount that squandered their capital in fruitless ventures. After all, the latter very rarely get a mention in mainstream investment publications.

Gold is an excellent leading indicator of expectations of inflation. Often Gold prices will adjust prior to the inflation occurring and can be viewed as a sign of the market's expectations of real interest rate adjustments. As Gold is non-perishable, much of the Gold that has ever been mined is held within inventories around the world. In light of this, Gold prices are likely to be decided by the expectations and beliefs of investors and central banks. If investors become aggregate sellers then the Gold price will respond negatively, the converse holds if investors aggregately increase their purchases. Gold allows the investor to diversify their portfolio, there is a degree of systemic risk which cannot be diversified away from an absolute equity portfolio, Gold can mitigate some of this risk.

Gold is allegedly an efficient hedge against crisis but this is far from certain. During the 1997 Asian financial crisis and the Russian default of 1998 Gold price movements were relatively flat. Generally speaking, Gold prices adjust more in line with confidence of currencies. Hence why a rise in interest rate is not guaranteed to suppress Gold prices. During the sterling crisis 1992 interest rates were iterated higher on a daily basis but sterling still crashed against other currencies. If interest rates are rising it could be seen that inflation is also rising, key indicators of this in coming years will likely be ascribed to protectionist measures by western governments. If tariffs are applied to Chinese imports or manufacturing jobs are re-shored to the US, the rise in production costs will be transmitted to the consumer. There is plenty of scenarios which could unfold to cause an inflationary effect.

Optimal timing of purchases will be desirable as the investor will be reliant on price movements to profit on precious metal holdings. Generally speaking, the best opportunities have presented themselves when the market was paying little interest to the activities of precious metal prices. The infamous 'Brown's Bottom' was arguably the best buying opportunity in several generations. This being at a time when the then Labour Party leader and Prime Minister Gordon Brown sold 400 tonnes of English Gold into the market at a twenty year low around the turn of the millennium. The price of Gold quadrupled thereafter in the proceeding decade.

The most prominent risk to the precious metals is a

rise in real interest rates. Two factors will act as a deadweight on real rates – the amount of debt exposure and the aging population. The age demographic in the west will likely coerce policy makers to hold nominal interest rates as low as possible. As any economist would tell you, the proportion of an individual's income that is saved tends to increase with one's age. We borrow more when young and save more when we are preparing for retirement. Given that people are living longer now it is plausible that they are saving more in the view of spending longer in retirement. With an ageing population, the paradox of thrift will show that the more people that are aggressively saving the worse it can be for the economy. Therefore, it is my view that interest rates will be held as low as possible to try to discourage households from saving too much whilst the economy is so feeble.

A final note on precious metals - many investors become overweight on Gold due to fear of currency depreciation. Stocks is another effective hedge against inflation and currency depreciation, in fact, many stocks yield a dividend payment which can be reinvested which shows that large holdings of Gold is not the only way to benefit from a fall in local exchange rates. It is very likely that a time will come in which a renewed bull market in Gold will entice more buyers into the market which are buying simply in reflection that prices have already risen. If the analyst concurs with this view they will accept that it is good practice to accumulate Gold over time much like a 'dollar-cost-averaging' stock portfolio.

Efficient Market Hypothesis

The efficient market hypothesis intimates that asset prices are a true reflection of all available information in the public domain. This statement assumes the following:

1) The market is an excellent valuation mechanism with only small gyrations about the true value

2) The market never allows the underlying assets to deviate from their inherent/potential value

3) Only inside traders can effectively forecast price movements before they materialize

Empirical observation will show us that this is not the case and that there exists many inefficiencies within the valuation process. Of course, if unforeseen fundamental developments occur then the asset price will be impacted greatly but I do not concur that asset prices are always a reliable true indicator to the value of the asset they are reflecting. The justification for this position is derived from investor sentiment. When market participants are bullish in respect to an asset, the price is often allowed to overshoot on the upside quite markedly. The same applies during panics in which selling pressures can cause asset valuations to become severely undervalued. The market effectively acts like a pendulum, over swinging in either direction dependent on market sentiment as investors adjust their outlooks based on what other investors are doing.

It follows then, that excellent buying and selling opportunities will present themselves. The difficulty can be recognizing when such an opportunity has presented itself. After all, a price fall in an equity of 20% may be a correction from a significant overvaluation, or could it be that this stock is now depressed and is presenting a buying opportunity? This dilemma is largely subjective and open to interpretation, it is only in hindsight that it becomes clear which postulate was valid. What clouds this judgement is our understanding of future business conditions and also the valuation of non-tangible assets such as branding.

Various strategies can be implemented in order to avoid such decision making. Markets can be volatile during periods of unrest and 'guessing' if a price swing is undervaluing an asset or merely correcting it can make a reliance on good fortune rather than excellent dexterity. If investors are pessimistic about a company its share price can be subdued for quite some time. When stock markets are entering bear markets, I tend to favor averaging purchases. There are various share accounts that allow for monthly purchases of stocks for very low transaction costs. I have found that this strategy helps reduce risk of mistiming share purchases and is very effective in declining markets. This method reduces the incidence of the investor jumping into the market with both feet at the wrong time. If the efficient market hypothesis is accurate in its description of how market prices adjust for events then what can be gained from following mainstream financial news stations? If the market has already interpreted the developments and revised valuations accordingly then the asset prices will be a full reflection of what is being broadcasted. If these events were foreseen then it is not unusual for prices to react contrarily to what one might expect, hence the 'buy on rumour – sell on news' mantra. Two exceptions to this ruling exist in the rare incidences of markets that anticipated events incorrectly and/or the emergence of a black swan event. The difficulty with appraising assets with information in the public domain is the counteracting nature of available data. It is simple to see how one can siphon through publications to find a case supporting an asset price but find other information that suggests the asset should be sold. For instance, an event that should cause a rise in oil prices will foster expectations of inflation which should be bullish for the price of Gold yet these expectations may cause central banks to raise interest rates which could be bearish for Gold. The investor should accept that it is very unlikely for an individual to consistently outperform the general market or to foresee the black swan events that will prove catalysts to large asset price revisions.

One of the gravest errors that investors can be inclined to make is to use an asset's market price as a bases for wholly appraising its inherent value. Demand for isolated assets is derived from what investors believe about the beliefs of other investors. As no investor is aware of the opinions of other market participants, he will make inferences based on the current market price of the asset. This sort of activity encourages herd-like behavior, investors are content at entering or adding to positions in appreciating environments because other investors seem to be doing the same thing. When there is a new publication of information it generates confusion as individuals are unsure how other market participants will respond. By basing their own judgements on the subsequent price movements, a spur of volatility is created as traders attempt to settle on a new equilibrium. It is often observed that trifling fundamental developments can cause marked swings in the asset price as investors attempt to second guess each others actions. Hence why many individuals would experience much better returns if they ignored the short term 'noise' of markets in a long term portfolio.

Investment Cash Flow

Retail investors have the option to purchase foreign exchange and foreign government bonds as a means of gaining exposure to these markets. There are many benefits to holding foreign exchange positions, such as the rapid appreciation of a currency after a peg being broken in addition to the value of certain currencies being loosely associated to commodity prices such as the Russian Ruble and Canadian Dollars link to crude oil. Like holding Gold, there is no cashflow when holding foreign reserves which makes them a higher risk investment. Companies that remit payments to their shareholders via dividends is an excellent tool for investing. If a company's share price depreciated after an investor purchases the stock, dividend reinvestment can ensure that the investment still produces a satisfactory yield.

There are some considerations when reviewing the dividend payments of individual equities in share portfolios that warrant inclusion in an investment book. Markets are very fickle when it comes to the revaluation of a stock after it increases or cuts its dividend payment. There is sometimes a political motive behind dividend strategies. It would seem that a company experiencing a reduction in profits would reduce its dividend to compensate this. Past observation has demonstrated to us that share prices can be punished by the market as soon as a dividend cut has been announced. Subsequently, many companies falling on hard times adopt a position of maintaining or even increasing their dividends. Why may this be and how should this be interpreted?

Plausible explanations for this stance are that directors may be adopting a longer term outlook when determining dividend policy or tolerating fluctuations on earnings before taking action. However, it could equally be part of an agency problem in which managers do not want to disappoint shareholders as it may lead to job insecurity. Thus they may decide to maintain dividends due to their own interests - even though they are aware it is harming the company's long term prospects. Furthermore, many institutional investors are reliant on dividend revenue streams for the functionality of their own business. This leaves the investor with the conundrum of which action to take in a situation where dividend payments are becoming an unsustainable liability for the company. One check that should always be made before the purchase of a security and on an annual basis thereafter is the status of the company's dividend cover ratio.

A dividend cover ratio can be a clear sign that the company's current dividend is becoming a financial burden particularly in high yield stocks. A dividend cover ratio of 1:1 shows that a company is remitting all of its profits to shareholders and not retaining any for future investment. A dividend cover ratio is denoted by:

Dividend Cover = after tax profit ÷ dividends
= earnings per share ÷ dividends per share

The Dividend cover ratio can hint to the sustainability of a dividend but it can also provide an insight of future increases in the dividend. If the ratio is increasing year-on-year then the company is better positioned to increase payments – with an increase in payments, the market will reevaluate the stock favorably.

Central Banks and Foreign Exchange

Since the 2009 stock market recovery one would be forgiven by claiming that asset prices have been decoupling from the fundamentals that they are supposedly reflecting. Stock markets are becoming far more sensitive to central bank policy and so it seems to me that central banks and their monetary policies are becoming the real drivers of markets. If a positive development occurs within the economy the stock market goes up, if negative events occur in the economy – the stock market goes up. As long as there is little movement on the expectations of interest rates then institutions are content at buying and holding large stock portfolios safe in the knowledge that central banks will interpose if price crashes develop. The housing market too is underpinned by favorable central bank policies – should these conditions change in any way then it could leave many property investors in negative equity. Some people may say 'but there are so many first time buyers that will snap up cheaper property' – this may hold for cash buyers but demand will be dictated by whether banks agree to lend. In a falling property market their balance sheets will be showing an increase in highly geared households across the board and falling valuations of the principle. I am not convinced they will want to rush into getting more highly leveraged mortgages, especially if unemployment is increasing, inter alia.

The issue with the actions that central banks employ is that it creates a series of ripple effects. If the Federal Reserve decides to embark on further money printing and lets the dollar depreciate against other currencies – it induces the other central banks to do the same. These other central banks may be forced into action due to pressure from several of their industries that claim they are becoming priced out of the international market due to the strength of the domestic currency. The consequences can be a ripple effect of activism in order to normalize FX rates. Of course, I accept that if the Dollar depreciates then the other currencies can maintain their relationship with one-another but for markets that are heavily dependent on US exports the effect that this has can be severe. However, making such generalizations can be dangerous in economics as this point of view is a very one-dimensional perspective. In practice, things are more complex than accepting that if a currency appreciates then exports will definitely suffer. For instance, large importers of raw materials will be able to buy more inputs for cheaper than rival firms based in other countries due to the stronger currency. This will render these firms more competitive. I have said many times in the past, a strong currency promotes efficiency. To add further weight to this viewpoint, if one focuses on Swiss Watch manufacturers - a $10,000 Swiss watch may have a production cost of $800 with the remainder attributed to marketing. So, whether the Swiss Franc tends up or down does not have any meaningful impact on the profitability of watch producers. In any event, currency fluctuations creates winners and losers.

The theme that can be identified from the interventionism of central banks is that there is excessive interference and much of the growth being observed is contingent growth that is reliant on an extrapolation of QE and low-interest rates - which cannot be sustained indefinitely. Of course, these actions are plausible in the short term immediately following a crisis but reliance on these measures has rendered the western world addicted to artificial demand from cheap and excessive liquidity. Central banks are becoming far too politically orientated with their policies being skewed by the incumbent government's own interests. I concede to the fact that we will probably see much lower interest rates than those of several decades ago, the world is a different place now. There are far too many imbalances being created by the reluctance to raise interest rates and my fear is that we will not know the full extent of these until it is too late.

6

INVESTMENT RISK

The complexity of global markets makes risk analysis extremely challenging as more information is available to us than we know what to do with. A well-known social science experiment was conducted in which participants were tasked with counting the amount of passes made by a group of individuals that were throwing a basketball to each other. During the short clip, someone dressed as a gorilla walks through the set. The findings were that the experiment participators were so fixed on the task that they did not notice the gorilla. The study highlights how something dramatic can be missed as the observers were too fixed on other things. In the perspectives of the market, with more indicators available than we know what to do with, it is simple to see how even the more experienced and educated analysts can fail to recognize danger.

This chapter will set out some of the theory that can be used in investment decisions from a risk perspective.

The Agency Problem

In the agency theory the shareholders, being the owners and principals of the company, are delegating the day to day running of the company to its directors and management, that is, the agents. A division emerges between control of the company and ownership. Should these separate parties act in their own interests, a situation may materialize in which conflicts of interest cause harm to the future of the company. Scenarios whereby there is a decoupling of the interests of managers and owners being when managers seek opportunities that increase their personal salaries even if the strategy is unlikely to be beneficial for the company. Similarly, managers may elect for options that ease their own workload such as appointing personal assistants or not taking on new business. Due to the presence of asymmetric information, the agent's actions are often not seen by shareholders. Therefore, company owners will need to monitor and interject in order to align the interests of the agents with themselves.

Similarly, shareholder interests can diverge from the interests in the management team as they have the privilege to diversify their holdings; having exposure to multiple companies. In this scenario, they could have a risk embracing attitude as they can diversify their risk and if desired, can exercise their option of divesting if a venture appears to be failing. Whilst it may be much harder for a manger to leave their post and occupy a similar position in another company. Therefore, it is simple to see how attitudes of risk exposure can cause conflict between the two parties.

As a shareholder, there is several avenues of opportunity to align respective interests to remedy the agency problem. At first glance, one could be applauded for suggesting incentives such as providing management with bonuses based on share options. However, this has the potential to encourage myopic attitudes which can be counterproductive over the longer-term. This is a particular consideration in a public listed company that is engaging in share buybacks. Is capital that can be used to develop the long-term prospects of the company being allocated to purchasing the company's shares in order for the share price to appreciate to a pre-agreed target that triggers bonuses for management? Furthermore, if managers are rewarded with free shares if the share price breaches a predetermined threshold; it can induce risk taking actions as managers receive all the rewards if a gamble pays off but are relatively immune to the downside if the venture does not perform as well as expected.

The agency problem can develop more freely in situations where the ownership of the company is relatively fragmented. Institutional investors that act on behalf of pension funds will have the ability to occupy a large proportion of company ownership affording them greater control of operations. Some of these said investors will favor approaches that lead to long term prosperity for the company; causing rejection of proposals that will cause short term gain for agents. A final note being that strictly speaking, as a shareholder, the management of the company work for you. Shareholder activism can overhaul a team of managers by exercising voting rights or opting for acceptance of takeover bids of the company. In my view, there is an adaptation of the agency theory which is contributing to anemic productivity. The benefits structure of many employment contracts is that the person fulfills a service and is remunerated a pre-agreed salary. In the absence of further incentives there can be a propensity for the employee to adjust their effort levels to that which is just sufficient to avoid attention of managers. Unless managers can incentivize staff in other ways, companies may be stuck in a scenario in which salaries are set at a price which is just enough to preclude staff from leaving the firm and employees put in just enough effort to not become subject to disciplinary action or dismissal. Measures should be taken to align interests of employees, their managers and the shareholders.

Investment Economics & Risk

Hammurabi Law and Bank Nationalization

The 2008 credit crisis sparked an uprising against parts of the banking sector after the public financed losses on the balance sheets of some of the largest financial entities after malfeasant attitudes had caused catastrophic losses. The investment banking sector had capsized the global financial system and taxpayers money was used to plug holes in balance sheets derived from a cocktail of excessive risk and leverage. Not one single charge was made against the senior board members of the Lehman Brothers institution, yet senior bankers in Iceland were later reprimanded by the Icelandic government and given prison sentences.

The fundamental issue with situations of this nature is that investment bankers were privileged to receive bonuses when large bets were placed that paid off. Whilst when they made risky punts that went against them they received nothing. There is an incentive, then, to take large risks as there is huge upside potential for success but the downsides have very limited accountability attached to them. At any time, if one has an asymmetric payoff, that is, you make more when you are right than you lose when you are wrong; excessive risk taking is encouraged.

Hammurabi's law is an ancient code that is traced back to the Babylonian King Hammurabi. He famously declared 'If a builder build a house for someone, and does not construct it properly, and the house which he built fall in and kill its owner, then that builder shall be put to death'[23]. Although this law can now be construe as being too primitive for the modern world; it demonstrates a culture of accountability which has been absent in modern times.

The architect of the house would be able to hide risk and will know more about the house than any regulator. Therefore to safeguard against asymmetric information that has potential to do harm onto others he should be held fully accountable. The applicability of this holds for financial products that were repackaged and sold on to investors during the period immediately prior to the 2008 financial crisis. An asymmetry of information allows for profiteering. A moral hazard attitude encourages reckless behavior when assessing risks. As necessitated by Hammurabi's law, accountability is the key ingredient to preventing a recurrence of the 2008 credit crisis.

Allowing bad banks to go bust would act as a deterrent for future bankers, however, consideration should be given to the interconnectedness of the banking industry. There is a severe risk that ethical and responsible banks would be at risk of a domino effect as capital markets recede and debts turn bad. Letting bad banks go bust could take down the responsible banks too. The solution, in my opinion, is to allow for taxpayers money to prop up some of the banks but the responsible participants in the bank's demise to be held fully accountable for their prior actions. This position was adopted by the Swedish government after they nationalized two banks in default. The respective CEOs and Chairmen of the Första Sparbank and Nordbanken were forced to resign in 1990 and 1991. Often commentators criticize those who endorse bank nationalization.

My view is that any state intervention should be done so in accordance with the interests of the taxpayers – if the bank represents a good investment then and only then should the public become embroiled in its affairs. In the event that the banks become publicly owned the management should be replaced. They failed once with their shareholder's money – they should not be afforded the same privilege with taxpayer's capital.

Risk in Overseas Investment

Owing to the fact that circa eighty percent of the World's population resides in emerging economies, and that many of these markets offer the lowest labor costs - many corporations have sought to prosper from relocating assets into these countries in a bid to enhance competitiveness. Whilst in many instances this has proven to be a plausible strategy, this process is fraught with risk. The most potent being political risk such as expropriation and governments reneging on categorical promises within contracts. As with the 'hold up' situation, governments can rescind bilateral agreements made with foreign companies that have begun investing in the domicile country. A foreign government's position strengthens with the intensity of the foreign firm's investments; as more sunk costs are committed to the operation; the firm stands to lose a larger amount if the government decides to negate any previous mutual agreements.

The one disincentive for governments acting in this manner is that it will act as a deterrent to future foreign investors. Caution should be exercised in an environment where high commodity prices have induced foreign firms to accept risks of investing in proven corrupt countries that have previously abused their foreign investors. An obvious example of this being oil exploration companies. Other factors to consider being that investing in foreign jurisdictions will necessitate the gathering of information and knowledge. Failure to comply with country specific legislation can result in penalization.

Emerging markets are susceptible to capital outflows induced by the reversal of loose monetary policies in market economies like the USA and the Eurozone. This will likely lead to a paradigm of defaults and payment crises. This, being particularly prominent in highly integrated regions as these are more susceptible to contagion. Examples of which being the Asia and the South American economies.

Foreign companies have followed various strategies in the past in order to keep the local authority on side. Investment in local causes such as infrastructure and contributing to the provision of public services such as educational programs has encouraged good relations with respective government officials and local communities alike. However, this is by no means a flaw proof strategy. Situations have previously arisen in which local communities have blocked mine egresses in a form of protest because of problems with a local provision that locals know has more chance of being addressed by a cash rich multinational company that the government. Hence why they direct their protests at foreign companies instead.

Portfolio Risk and Decisional Bias

If flaws in the human subconscious was found to distort the decision making process, then one can safeguard themselves against making poorly informed decisions when forming or readjusting an investment portfolio. Empirical studies have found that people employ a certain set of rules when making judgements in risk – these being known as heuristics. Although conceptual in nature, the below traits are important considerations for any investor.

1) **Representativeness**: Individuals believe that if more information is provided there is more chance of something being true. There is an illusion that more detail provides greater insight whereas the more specific a scenario the less chances there are of it occurring.

2) **Availability** – when asked to estimate the frequency of an event or the probability of an event people will assume the probability is greater if they can easily remember an instance of the event. This would suggest that investors scorned from a bear market may fail to recognise and capitalise on low market valuations as they have vivid memories of stocks continuously falling.

Availability is a misleading indicator of frequency. If an event can be easily retrieved from memory it will result in probability being overestimated. The ease in which something can be imagined also influences decision making. Implicitly, then, following financial news can skew your own thought process. With the majority of the investment community watching the same news stations as each other one has to question the merit of obtaining information from these channels if it induces everybody to be simultaneously bullish or bearish.

3) **Adjustments and anchoring** – this occurs when individuals are asked to make an estimate of some object. Typically, people will start with the initial guess which acts as an anchor. This may be based on the original question formulation and then adjusted as the individual is given more data, typically the adjustments are small.

4) **Failure of Hindsight** – features an agent's inability to learn from the past. The notion is adequately described as the ' I knew that was going to happen' effect with the agent believing that their ability to manage past events is higher than it actually was. This is said to diminish their ability to learn from past events. An example of this may be that an oil

major such as Chevron fails to recognise their risk exposure to a deep sea well blowout similar to BP because they believe that the event was specific to how BP operate and so is less likely to happen to them. Further, events such as the 2008 crash appear more obvious in hindsight and so we may believe that something so obvious to us now would be easily foreseeable.

5) **The Groupthink effect** – when decision making is performed as part of a group it can lead to an illusion of invulnerability and over-optimism. There are many reasons as to why this occurs such as pressure being directed towards any group member who dissents from the majority view. Further, staff can feel intimidated in revealing that their views are not consistent with that of a high profile staff member. Companies can safeguard against Groupthink by appointing a devil's advocate to challenge convention and also allowing lower ranked staff members to present their ideas first.

Generally speaking, humans are considered poor rational decision makers. They disregard base rates when estimating probabilities, overestimate their own ability to take control and commit to sunk cost fallacy in which they continue to invest in failure because they have done so in the past. They take undue credit for their achievements, which is an important consideration as some results will be a product of variation. They are reluctant to accept self-inflicted failures and ignore the limits of data available to them.

To truly comprehend the limitations of our misconceptions of probability, if one was to flip a coin six times, which outcome seems more likely?

H denotes Heads and T denotes Tails:

1) **THHTHT**

2) **TTTTTT**

The results are of course equiprobable outcomes yet most individuals would likely assume that given the arbitrary nature to the first set of results - it makes it a more likely outcome. There are further subconscious decisional bias anomalies to which we are exposed to that will be duly outlined in the following subsections.

The Endowment Effect

The endowment effect intimates that an individual will request a higher price in order to sell an item than they would be willing to pay for the item themselves. In effect, their ownership of the item has caused them to overvalue it. The justification being that the disutility of relinquishing the item is greater than the utility of acquiring it in the first instance. The theory was initially observed in a series of experiments but it is plausible to suggest that this decisional bias is applicable to portfolio investments in which investors become 'attached' to certain holdings in their portfolio. This could cause property investors to hold onto real estate for longer than they should or stock investors to become effectively married to positions despite them offering attractive selling prices.

The Loss Aversion Theory

I first came across this doctrine when researching factors that influence decisions on whether firms retain risks or transfer them by purchasing insurance policies. The theory is largely concerned with distinguishing between risk embracing and risk aversion attitudes. It is said that the emotional pain that a person incurs from suffering a loss is double the pleasure of making a respective gain[24]. This, understandably, has huge implications for managing an investment portfolio and explains why so many investors sell their shares near the bottom of down moves in the market. The distress of a share portfolio depreciating in a bear market can trick one's mind into distress selling when the market is actually attractively valued.

The preference to avoid losses relative to making an equivalent gain can explain why investors can be reluctant to buy shares that have been in an established bear market. The thought of further losses can encourage inertia at least until they see the stock have a meaningful rally. The loss aversion phenomena is a key reason to why I rarely review the share prices of the companies that I am invested in. I am aware of the fallacies that I am innately exposed to and years of investing have confirmed that by only loosely following these share prices, I can almost completely preclude selling assets at precisely the wrong time.

Winners Curse

This theory is less specific to portfolio theory but I wish to borrow it for further evidence of flaws in investment decision making. The Winners curse is central to auctions and posits that the winning bid in an auction will be in excess of the true intrinsic value of the item. This makes sense because in effect the individual that bids the highest for an item is the one that overvalues the item the most. One could suggest that the true intrinsic value resides close to the median bid. The median is chosen here as it is not distorted by outliers (extreme values) like the arithmetic mean would be. This theory demonstrates two things; that when valuing an asset there is a general divergence in opinion which allows for error and also that some of this decision making is likely distorted by emotion. Both of these befit the investment decision making process.

The Survivorship Bias

This decisional bias stems from the false representation of results from a given sample. This is a common assumption error in which the odds of success are heavily skewed due to a failure to take the sample size into account. One could be forgiven if after watching a documentary based on five FX traders that all own supercars and mansions that FX trading will make you rich. However, one should only make these assumptions if the same size is known, that is: how many others partook in the same trading career but did not feature on the documentary? If 30,000 people started to trade and all of them became rich then the initial hypothesis that trading will enrich you is quite plausible. However, if the 30,000 individuals partook in the same trading career and all but five lost their money, would you still be inclined to make the same conclusion? It is the lack of sample size quantification that allows us to make false conclusions on the probabilities of success due to sampling error. This is mainly compounded by the fact that only the successful individuals are represented, the losers do not make the TV documentary.

Furthermore, there can be false conclusions drawn from 'success stories' of individuals that have been successful at business ventures, market predictions or wealth creation. I would like to make explicit that even with overwhelming evidence to suggest that the individual is a guru or an expert in their field, the analyst should refrain from becoming fooled by track records of this sort. If you arbitrarily selected fifty children and gave them £10,000 to invest in the markets, by variation alone one may expect at least one of the children makes a fortune whilst the others fail.

The instant reaction is to attribute this to the child's excellent business acumen and economic foresight but this could also be a function of randomness. After all, he prospered when all others failed. The same holds for market analysts. If there are enough 'experts' giving their opinions of the market in televised interviews then murphy's law dictates that eventually one of them will accurately foresee a significant event. If an analyst predicts a crisis enough then invariably one day he will be proven correct. Of course some individuals are better positioned to succeed that others but let's not forget the powerful influence of variation in the results that we observe.

The survivorship bias is particularly potent amongst speculators concerning themselves with penny shares. It is easy to judge potential reward on a handful of successes rather than a wealth of duds.

Confirmation Bias

A cognitive observation in the decision making process is said to exist in which humans are selective over how they process information according to their pre-existing entrenched beliefs. 'Confirmation bias' is an information processing error in which an individual may purposefully search for and interpret information to confirm their existing thoughts. I have observed in the precious metals community, investors often try to locate information that is bullish for Gold prices even when most reports suggest on the contrary.

It is simple to see why one can be motivated to do this when they are overweight a particular asset class. It seems we seek comfort in sorting information to justify the decisions that we have made or wish to make. One is said to be more likely to recall and translate information to solidify their existing bias. This systemic processing error extends to technical analysis of price charts. These can be largely subjective with many conflicting signs leaving there a risk that the analyst may look for signs embedded in the chart that confirms their position. Having awareness of this phenomena can help safeguard against it. It is particularly important if one has a large holding in a company as any new reports could contain warning signs which the analyst must be free from any incentive to 'cherry-pick' information rather than critically analyzing.

In sum, availability has the largest influence as it is frequently employed; especially since media related images make it easier for us to recall disastrous events and increase the probability of them occurring, in our minds at least. Studies have also demonstrated that most people believe they are less at risk than the average person, statistically this simply cannot be the case. This 'optimum bias' can be difficult to insulate oneself from as it is open to interpretation as to if one is disproportionately optimistic or being rational. However, it may be useful for the investor to remind themselves to form investment decisions not based on the probability of being correct, but the risk of being wrong. No matter how confident one is about a given prospect, you should always question how your portfolio will be affected if your analysis is proven incorrect. The analyst should acknowledge these behavioral biases and accept that one's judgement can be clouded by subconscious fallacies that are difficult to suppress.

The Boiling Frog Syndrome

This theory uses the metaphor of a boiling frog to show the dangers of continuity in unsustainable situations. It is claimed that a frog placed in a pan of water will not bestir itself if the water is heated gradually overtime. The frog is said to be unable to detect the danger as it is too comfortable with continuity to realize that continual change at a point will become intolerable and necessitate a change in environment. Although conceptual in nature, this principle applies to the investment community as small iterative changes are dismissed by the public whom are too comfortable with current themes to notice underlying dangers. The boiling frog syndrome acts as a reminder to deploy a critical and curious mind when assessing markets. It is conceivable that the sovereign debt levels seen in some of the western economies are subject to the boiling frog syndrome. Arguably, this phenomena plays a significant role in the unsustainability of currency pegs, showing that taking comfort in continuity could lead to crisis at a later date.

Bookmakers, Insurance and the Law of Large Numbers

When studying probability theory I stumbled across a theorem that is very applicable to the insurance and gambling markets. The axiom explains how insurers can accurately price risk and how bookmakers should always profit over the longer-term. When multiple events occur with the same likelihood of success there is a convergence between actual and expected results as the number of trials increases. Put simply, if one flips a coin three times there is a fair chance that they produce three heads. However, if one was to flip the coin one-hundred times we would expect that the amount of heads registered will be similar to the number of tails, given the equiprobable outcomes of a coin flip.

In the view of bookmakers, the results from betting on future events may deviate from what is considered standard and expected in the short term. For instance, there can be a higher than expected amount of winning bets but over the longer-term one can expect that there is a convergence between the actual and expected performance of bets. Insurers use the same logic as they know that if there is one claim for every seventy insurance policies that are sold - they can expect any anomalous results in the near term will normalize to the expected values as more policies are sold. The law of large numbers suggests that as the number of trials tends to affinity, the underlying probability of an event occurring conforms closer to its expected value. The single exception being when the odds are distorted by a rare low predictability high impact event.

Black Swan Events

Prior to the discovery of Australia, common consensus had no reason to believe that swans were any other color but white. The sighting of a single black bird destroyed the firmly held belief that all swans were white. This logic transmitted into the world of investment that one cannot rule out the existence of a black swan just because he has not seen one before.

Therefore, you may often hear the term 'black swan' used frequently by market commentators. The expression being used to describe a statistical outlier that was unforeseeable based on past observation. These rare events have taken many forms throughout history such as breakthrough inventions, wars and medical discoveries. The rise of Hitler, discovery of electricity, the sinking of the Titanic and the 9/11 terrorist attacks were all respective black swan events. For classification purposes, black Swans lie outside the scope of expectations because nothing in the past can hint to their possibility. These events carry an extreme impact and are of low predictability by nature - if they were predictable then it is questionable as to if they would ever have happened.

The important lesson that Black Swans deliver is that we function on an illusion of knowledge, we believe that we understand the world that we live in when in fact, it is much more complex and random that we realize. Ben Bernanke, the then chairman of the Federal Reserve; was quoted in 2005 during a televised interview in response to economists claiming that house prices were in a bubble and a crash of their prices could cause a recession. He presupposed that 'It's a pretty unlikely possibility, we have never had a decline in house prices on a nationwide basis, so what I think is more likely is that house prices will slow and maybe stabilize'[25].

The basis for his argument being that this scenario was unlikely because it had not happened before. His error was not that he was ill-informed, or lacking intellectual capacity but presumably because he based his predictions on past trends. On balance of evidence he was probably correct in what he stated was the most likely scenario but things do not function on the weighing up of evidence all the time. Every now and then a black swan reminds us how limited our understanding of the world is and investors that are not sufficiently diversified or overleveraged are exposed to the biggest loses, generally speaking.

The Black Swan Problem and Oil Company Insurance Strategies

There are few better examples of the magnitude of a black swan event than the 2010 Macondo well blowout. British Petroleum (BP) owned a 65% share of the 'well from hell'. BP had decided, based on past performance, to self-insure against losses incurred from incidents derived from its hydrocarbon exploration and extraction. The reason for this being multifold; high frequency low impact incidents were covered by many insurers. This meant that existing infrastructure could cover these risks efficiently and resulted in a competitive priced market. In light of this – BP decided to purchase insurance for low impact claims as these insurance products were economically attractive.

Low frequency high impact events are difficult to foresee and so not many insurers offer cover for this which results in an uncompetitive market. Consequently, this sort of risk transfer mechanism is expensive. Given that BP had determined that insurance premiums paid in the last decade markedly exceeded losses recovered. They decided to self-insure exposures over $10 million. This was largely based on the assumption that the future would look like the past.

Other factors would have been considered in this decision making process such as BP being financially larger than many of the insurers that offered this type of financial indemnification. Furthermore, BP knew its risks better that any underwriter which would allow for optimization of pricing of risk. There was a consensus that BP was being charged the industry rate and not afforded the recognition that was deserves for superior safety standards. BP's main error being that assumptions based on extrapolation of the past are subject to major error as they do not account for black swan events. As we now know, the eventual consequence of the incident was catastrophic and resulted in astronomical losses.

There is facility for similar incidents occurring in the future in deep well reservoirs and despite the catastrophic loss when the well blowout occurred,

BP's 2016 annual report states '…BP generally purchases insurance only in situations where there is legally and contractually required. We typically bear losses as they arise rather than spreading the over time through insurance premiums'[26]. Like BP, many oil majors are operating under a 'captive insurance' practice. This involves forming an insurance company whose business is supplied and dictated by its owners to finance risks from its parent company. Simply put, captives are insurers that are owned by the insured that finance their owner's risk.

If an oil rig operator were to seek commercial insurance they would be subject to appeasing the maritime survey warranty which is a supervisory exercise in which the insurer can nullify the insurance contract agreement if it is found that the rig operator is not complying with safety standards. This allows the insurer to certify that the rig operator is adhering to international regulations. Rig operators can waiver this safety check by forming their own captive insurance company, in turn, allowing for the safety standards to be determined at the rig operators discretion.

Further, offshore companies can register their Mobile Offshore Drilling Unit (MODU) under a flag of convenience which would not be allowed under a conventional insurance agreement. This allows the operator to bypass regulatory standards that would otherwise be mandatory under a conventional insurance agreement. Operating with a captive insurance setup and a flag of convenience, MODUs can operate under very little or the complete absence of any supervisory activities. This brings into question whether the industry is heading towards another well blowout disaster. Interestingly, as already mentioned, BP would have based decisions on how to manage their risk on past data, the problem of induction shows how handicapped this approach can be.

The Problem of Induction

If one is studying rare events; you will not have much empirical sample data to study. A one-hundred-year hurricane happens once every hundred years, if you have sixty years of data you will not see it. Rare events are not predictable empirically as you will require more data that is available, this assumes that you believe that the past is relevant of course! It is important to recognize that risk is in our future and not in our past. Reviewing past trends is not a gateway to foreseeing the future. A black swan highlights the limitations that we have from learning from history. Fabricating assumptions based on current knowledge can be subject to massive miscalculation. History repeatedly shows us that things that have not happened before do happen and so we cannot accurately make inferences about future events based on what we have previously observed. Accepting this theory at face value may lead the reader to pontificate the value of attempting to make forecasts if we consider our knowledge base as contingent. However, we need not neglect our previous experiences but we must accept the need for recognizing the limitations of the past when predicting the future. Accounting for black swan events is the chief justification for a well-diversified portfolio and a reserve of cash in case of an unexpected event causing massive disruption to one's assets.

Naïve Diversification and Risk Mitigation

Many companies are diversifying their revenue streams to hedge against loss incurred from a disruption to their business. A simplistic illustration of this would be a company that makes summer garden furniture. This would likely experience a cyclical demand trend. A summer of adverse weather could cause the business to incur serious loss for the year. By diversifying their product range, they can hedge against a reduction in demand of their seasonal products. An example of this diversification effort being Tesco. They operate primarily as a supermarket chain; however, they also operate Tesco Bank and their own mobile phone network. Investors should place this into consideration when appraising a company. It is not unreasonable for companies to purchase smaller firms that have no connection to their existing brand, this is simply diversifying revenue streams and should generally be viewed as a positive tactic. This should not be confused with companies that make several acquisitions per annum and go on to later sell them off at a loss.

Diversification works best when risks of one project is offset by another's. For example, some businesses are susceptible a fall in the domestic exchange rate, an example being cruise companies. If they are selling tickets to Spanish customers travelling to the Caribbean - if the Euro falls against the Dollar then the company, ceteris paribus, will experience a fall in profits as its revenue will be in Euros yet its costs will be primarily in dollars. The group could purchase a company that manufactures goods in the Eurozone that exports primarily to America. Any fall in the Euro/Dollar exchange rate will result in a relative increase in profit as their costs will be in euros and their profits in dollars. A company that can spread its operations between several projects can generally reduce risk. Naïve diversification is a strategy in which projects are combined in equal proportions to mitigate risk of the company.

One of the best insurance policies against serious portfolio loss of principle is effective diversification. Some investors may believe they are adequately diversified by investing in companies from different sectors. Whilst this demonstrates a basic level of diversification, it leaves the investor overweight in a single stock market. It is a misconception that risk can be completely diversified away, a brief explanation of risk nature will be necessary to comprehend this notion.

The composition of risk takes two forms, specific and systematic.

- **Specific risk** relates to a particular activity or business venture.

This form of risk can be diversified by spreading investments across multiple projects. If one project becomes sub-par, the other projects have facility to offset this by outperforming expectations. Intuition suggests that selecting multiple small scale projects rather than a single large project will convey a lower level of risk.

- **Systemic risk** relates to exogenous factors such as cyclical economic trends, interest rate adjustments or government policy changes.

This type of risk is considered to be generally immune from diversification as it represents inherent risk of doing business and affects the entire market. In sum, diversification can be employed to reduce specific risk but will have very limited influence on systemic risk. Specific risks are significantly reduced as diversification increases. Fosbeck (1985) intimated that specific risk can be reduced by 93 percent in a portfolio that includes 16 different stocks. This claim was made on the assumption that each holding was of equal weighting[28].

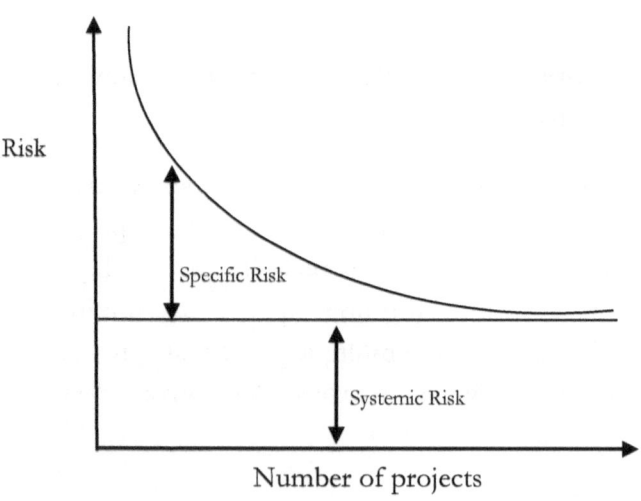

This risk model shows the benefits and limitations of diversification. There is an exponential reduction in risk as the number of projects is increased – however - the effect tapers markedly as the benefits of diversification are exhausted. Systemic risk is immune to diversification and remains a constant irrespective of how well distributed assets are.

Risk is best tempered when a portfolio combines securities that share a low or negative covariance. For instance, if an investor occupied a holding in an oil producing equity and the price of oil fell, their portfolio would have the potential to offset some of this risk if they owned stock in an airline company as lower oil pricing will reduce costs for airline companies. As aforementioned, one can diversify their investments but also diversify the timing of their purchases which can further mitigate some risk of being overexposed prior to downside market corrections.

Entering Emerging Markets – Risk

There are numerous considerations for the firm that wishes to expand into an emerging economy; namely methods, scale and timing. The notion of a firm expanding into an emerging market is an exciting prospect and a substantial risk vs reward dilemma. During my studies in risk I produced many reports of strategic entry of MNCs into emerging economies. The following acts as a guide as to the factors that should be considered.

The timing of transitioning into a new market is a consideration that must not be overlooked. Entry can be deemed as 'early' when a firm moves into a foreign market before other foreign firms. Exercising this strategy can provide the enterprise with a 'first mover advantage'. This being the ability to pre-empt rivals and absorb demand by establishing a branding. In turn, this will allow the firm to increase sale volume and transition down the experience curve ahead of rivals and gain a cost advantage over later entrants. Dependent on the nature of the firm, they may be able to tie customers into contracts so that if a rival firm competes for customers it may make it difficult for them to win business.

However, there is a downside to being the first firm to attempt to break into a new market. There is likely to be pioneering costs associated with tapping into new markets that later entrants will be able to avoid. Examples being the cost of business failure should the firm make major mistakes due to lack of consumer understanding. Different cultures may need to be educated to the value of the firm's products or services which will likely be borne by the first market entrant.

The scale of entry is something that can be vital to success of the venture. Firms that make substantial investment are making a strategic commitment that may distort the dynamics of the market. The gravity of these investments will have a long-term impact and ae very difficult to reverse. The expression 'throwing good money after bad' is a phase that justified Tesco's withdrawal from the USA at a cost of £1.2 billion[29]. A small-scale entry can be desirable as it allows firms to learn about the foreign market and in the process, limit the amount of exposure that it has to that market.

The method of entry is arguably the decision that necessitates the most consideration as so many viable options are available. Exporting being the most obvious choice. This is relatively low cost and allows the firm to achieve experience curve economies. The downside to exporting being the potential presence of a lower-cost manufacturing location. Transport costs may erode profit margins and the firm may become exposed to trade embargos and/or tariff barriers.

A tact that is often overlooked by management teams is the Turnkey project. This features a contractor that agrees to manage a project on behalf of a foreign client. Including sourcing of equipment and staff. At the completion of the contract, the foreign client is handed the 'key' to a facility that is now in operation. Turnkey projects allow firms to benefit from local knowledge required to assemble and operate a technologically complex process. Turnkey projects should not be attempted if the firm's process technology is a source of competitive advantage.

A common tactic in the Pharmaceutical sector is licensing. This being an arrangement in which a firm lends intangible property such as patent rights, trademarks, inventions and processes to another agent for a predetermined time frame, in return, receiving a royalty. Favoring this method of expansion will allow the firm to bypass any development costs and risks associated with entering a new market. It provides another opportunity for owners of intangible assets to monetize these without further contributing to its production. The risk in this strategy being that the firm will not have control over manufacturing or marketing which would have otherwise allowed it to benefit from experience curve and location economies. There is significant risk of loss of proprietary property in this process. To mitigate this, firms often agree to form joint ventures with the featured party.

Joint Ventures and Acquisitions

Joint ventures are a common tactic employed by firms of various magnitudes. There will be plenty of opportunities to invest in companies that have formed joint ventures or partook in acquisitions. This subsection will introduce this activity and share an overview of the risk and reward trade-off.

A joint venture is the establishment of a firm that is jointly owned by two or more independent companies. This can allow a firm to benefit from a foreign company's local knowledge, culture and language. This will act as a risk reduction mechanism as the costs of setting up in a new market will be distributed between the participating enterprises.

Having a foreign partner in business may reduce the risk of 'hold up' situations developing in which governments change agreements after a foreign company has made investments in a project in their country. This could include appropriating assets such as oil fields or gem mines. If investing in a firm that is engaged in a joint venture agreement, a factor to consider is that the company risks another company gaining insight into its technology and processes. A reason for the rapid development of the Chinese manufacturing sector was that foreign companies were required to enter into joint ventures with

Chinese firms if they wanted to do business in China. This allowed Chinese firms to imitate processes that may have taken years of trial and error to develop. Shared ownerships can facilitate growth for emerging economy's companies but can result in conflicts if mutual objectives change overtime.

At the time of writing, the incidence of cross border acquisitions is increasing. In the last decade, over half of all foreign direct investments have been mergers and acquisitions. Acquisitions can be completed relatively quickly and enable firms to pre-empt their rivals in emerging markets. However, many acquisitions are not successful for a variety of reasons. The most obvious being that the acquirer appraises the assets of the acquired firm too generously. A clash of cultures may materialize between the two enterprises causing a breakdown of goodwill. Lastly, if insufficient pre-acquisition screening was conducted then the purchase could turn sour shortly after the deal is done as underlying issues emerge.

Board of Directors and Risk Management

Although this topic lays outside the conventional realms of economics, it is a very important and often overlooked consideration that investors should be mindful of when reviewing individual securities. As the Enron and Tesco debacles have demonstrated to us, a poor quality board of directors (BOD) can wreak havoc on share prices. There is very little an individual shareholder can do to determine if a BOD are acting in the true interests of the company or not, however, there are several good practices which will be briefly summarized.

Companies that allow for the amalgamation of the chairman and CEO positions can result in an unhealthy concentration of power. Therefore, it is recommended that the chairman and CEO positions are separated to prevent any one individual from being afforded unfettered influence on the decision making process. Lest we forget that it is the board's decision to determine the remuneration that the CEO receives. If the CEO is also the chairman, they are able to vote on their own pay which demonstrates a clear conflict of interests.

To prevent a BOD turning a company run by mangers into one being run for managers; Non-Executive Directors (NEDs) play an important role in observing and advising the BOD from a shareholders perspective. They are the eyes and ears of shareholders and should exercise their persuasive position to block any agentic endeavors by other directors. Their independence status is vital and anything less could be construe as an accident waiting to happen. As became apparent with Enron, the NEDs had severe conflict of interests which removed their independence. It can be regarded as good practice for NEDs to be afforded a fair salary for the time and resources that they bring to the BOD but not to participate in share options or pension schemes. Ideally there will be a rotation of NEDs that does not allow for excessively long tenures within the board. What one deems as 'excessive' in this circumstance is understandably subjective.

The constituents of a BOD should change in reflection of new challenges faced by the company but one should always question the initial appointment method and length of service for NEDs. Company presentations often parade past achievements of NEDs like crown Jewels on display, but this amounts to very little value for the company if the NEDs are drinking buddies with the CEO and were appointed to the company's board over a couple of rounds of golf and a few pints in the local pub. An investor should identify any companies that are adopting a 'jobs for the boys' mindset and avoid them at all costs.

The Relationship Between Risk and Innovation

Innovation creates change and the expansion of the knowledge horizon which harbors risk of undesirable outcomes. Innovation is often a nonlinear process conveying multiple iterations along a development path as difficulties are faced. Risks are an inherent component of innovation as success is not a given certainty. The incidence of an innovation often both creates and destroys in a uneven fashion, some companies may lose their customers to a rival innovator but wealth is created elsewhere due to technological change being deployed. Not all innovations are disruptive however. Incremental innovations are gradual as new processes are sought to improve dynamics of the business process.

It is irrefutable that the successful implementation of a new technology has potential to create an unforeseen and undesirable outcome which was not factored into the initial model. This has the ability to lead to a catalogue of subsequent risks causing a permeation of undesirable consequents. An example of which being asbestos, the substance successfully fulfilled its purpose as an insulating agent, however has since been deemed a causal factor in many chronic medical conditions.

Other scenarios may materialize in which the successful implementation of a new technology may be disruptive in nature leading to the detriment of others. An example being the adoption of an automated process, causing an adverse effect on human resources such as staff morale and talent retention as workers resist change and leave.

Some innovations can reduce or mitigate existing risks, an example being safety equipment in motor vehicles such as airbags, thus reducing the risk of severe injury during a collision. Other forms of innovation have potential to exacerbate pre-existing risks, leverage instruments on financial securities being an excellent example. This can come as no fault to the original pioneer. Some industries have stemmed from the evolution of a single idea and manifested into a sector that is riddled with risk, an example being cybercrime on the world wide web. It is simple to see how a situation like this can arise, some new technologies are invented with limited information available to the innovator. In this circumstance, there may be very limited data to inform decisions and the knowledge that is considered to be reliable may transpire to be inaccurate or in need of significant revision.

A specific risk to consider from innovation is the potential harm to the reputation of an enterprise's management team from loss attributed to a failed project or business venture. Starting a new business is a high-risk exercise as it is estimated that half of all businesses fail within their first three years[30]. Reputational risk occurs when organizations fall short of their stakeholders' expected standards. Intangible assets such as brand and reputation are earned from previous successes. When a firm experiments with new ventures, it exposes its branding and reputation to criticism and damage. An overcautious board of directors may place their reputation in such high regard that it impedes opportunities to reach into new markets or products. Thus reinforcing the notion that inertia is not a risk averse strategy.

The value of brand and reputation should never be underestimated. The acquisition of Rowntrees by Nestle brought this to light as when one adds up ten times Rowntrees' profits, the sum doesn't even come to half of what Nestle paid. The significance of this deal being that Nestle was capable of manufacturing anything that Rowntrees produced; leading one to conclude that the £2.3billion paid for Rowntrees was largely for their brands. Reputation begets trust and although a shortage of cash can bring a company to its knees, it is frequently the loss of the company's reputation that deals the final blow[31]. As Cowton (2009) posits, '….money might make the world go round, but one of the things that has been learnt from watching emerging economies is that trust makes it go round far better'[32]. As these accounts demonstrate - one should never underestimate the value of a company's reputation and branding.

The Success Breeds Failure Syndrome

Andrew Grove, the past CEO of Intel once said 'Success breeds complacency. Complacency breeds failure. Only the paranoid survive'. There is significant merit to this statement and history repeats with many organizations succumbing to their inability to adapt to change. It is not the company's resources or track records that determine their long term prosperity but their ability to transition and evolve. As Charles Darwin famously stated 'It is not the strongest of the species that survives, nor the most intelligent that survives. It is the one that is the most adaptive to change'. This methodology summarizes the need for portfolio revision over the longer term, some sectors are more prone than others to how adaptive they need to be. Technology is an obvious example. Individuals that invested in Nokia or Kodak will not need any further reminding about the importance of adaptation over time. The notion behind the success breeds failure syndrome is past success is construe as confirmation that the company is safe and robust. Success causes surging share prices, managerial bonuses, ease in recruiting the best talent in the industry and rivals responding with flattering attempts to imitate which further compounds complacency. It follows from this analysis that building a successful business can be much easier than maintaining one.

This was evident in the UK Supermarket sector. The 'big four' – Asda, Sainsburys, Tesco and Morrisons enjoyed their respective market shares with business models that didn't vary too much from year to year. German companies Aldi and Lidl expanded into the UK market and changed the playing field. Their new low cost and simplistic business models captured market share from the big four. Simple but effective changes were implemented – multiple and larger barcodes were placed on packaging to increase speed at the checkouts, produce is brought into the store and left on pallets which reduced labor costs and the supply chain was condensed to further reduce costs. As previously mentioned, breaking into an oligopoly is a very lucrative achievement. The response of the big four was a subsequent race to the bottom in cutting margins to try to fend off competition and defend market share from the German low cost producers. The market saw what was happening and the share prices of the three UK listed supermarkets was punished.

There was an air of complacency which likely stemmed from strong performance in the past; strategies that worked so well previously started to fail as business conditions changed. The confidence past successes convey to a company can reduce the recognition that change is warranted in order to survive over the longer-term. Some of the star performers of stock markets can be particularly monolithic and unresponsive to a change in environment. I am an advocate of the 'buy and hold' strategy with investments but even this has its limitations. The success breeds failure syndrome shows us that complacency can lead to a fall from grace. Investors should monitor their long term portfolios for companies showing signs of complacency and reluctance to tinker with their business to adapt and capitalize on new technologies.

Past performance has a significant influence on future strategies in more ways than just causing complacency. The perceived performance of an organization will have an influence on its risk appetite. Enterprises with a substandard performance will seek risk - non-performing companies have a negative correlation between risk and return – as their income reduces their risk is increased. Whereas, companies that recognize their above industry average performance will look to evade risk. Such firms will have a positive correlation towards risk and return.

Implicit in this view, if a company performs better than expected then it will likely continue its operations as before. However an underperforming company will seek ways to improve. There are two methods a firm can employ to measure performance. They can benchmark themselves against the industry average or a rival - alternatively they can measure themselves against their own past performance. Risk taking behaviors increase as the firm falls further below industry average. This heightened risk appetite often leads to lowered subsequent performance. Many will be familiar with the alleged linear relationship between risk and reward – significantly increase your risk and you may significantly increase your reward. By increasing risk in this way, one could significantly increase their losses. Whilst it may hold that high risk is necessary for large profits - it is equally required for large losses.

Risk and Regulation

Each new financial crisis attracts further calls for more regulation. Whilst this may be useful in some situations it is burdensome in others. If, for instance, regulators imposed a lending ceiling on banks in order to preclude them from becoming overexposed; banks may respond by seeking other methods to maximize profits. In effect, innovating to circumvent the restrictions imposed onto them. An example of this being that banks engaging in merging activities in order to exploit economies of scale. If regulations are restricting the amount they can profit from lending practices then entering into a joint venture with a rival bank will allow each of them to close bank branches due to duplication. Instead of two independent bank branches in the same town, they can merge and close one of the branches which will significantly reduce costs.

In spite of the fact that regulators have reduced the leverage ratio of the bank – they have incentivized the smaller banks to form larger entities. Further, we have seen many times in the past where strict regulations have given banks little reason to develop advanced risk analysis and contingency plans. The controls in place are ones forced onto them by regulators so they have little incentive to employ expensive risk analysts. Any subsequent deregulation and derestriction in lending often proves to be an accident waiting to happen as the banks are ill prepared for the liberties afforded to them by revoking lending ceilings. This was a large contributory factor to the Swedish banking crisis in the 1990s.

7
———

CLOSING COMMENTS & PREDICTIONS

Scenario Analysis

An increasingly evident paradigm when exchanging views with investors is that individuals tend to devote a large amount of time and research into a company when deciding on whether to buy its stock. However, once an owner, the investor becomes content with their prior research and they demonstrate complacency that the hard work is now over. This could not be further from the truth.

A technique for forecasting employed by risk managers and analysts is 'scenario analysis'. This scenario planning is conducted by bank and insurance regulators for purposes of 'stress testing' and is also utilized by large corporations such as Royal Dutch Shell. In the case of the banking regulators - the robustness of financial institutions is predicted by a series of scenario projections. Most frequently, the means of conducting this type of analysis is running simulations of future crisis situations and conducting contingency plans accordingly.

The process itself involves the identification of possible scenarios in which alternative futures are identified that are not merely extrapolations of current trends. This may feature the identification of new rivals into the market, after all past observation has frequently reminded us that the most significant competitors have often emerged from unexpected sources in surprising circumstances. This form of analysis is not confined to new entrants, long-term rival firms can employ strategies that are out of character with their conventional operations. The investor should explore a series of different pathways into alternative futures that the market is not expecting in order to prepare their portfolio for potential black swan events.

We know by the efficient market theorem that asset prices are designed to reflect all known information; therefore the rewards from premeditating potential adverse developments can be extremely fruitful. Could the advancement of fracking and subsequent crash in oil prices in 2016 have been projected by a series of 'what if' scenarios? Gordon Brown selling half of the UK's Gold reserves based on past trends could have been averted in a series of alternative future projections was considered. Many scenarios could have been projected in which Gold prices could have risen substantially.

In these alternative scenarios, analysts should concern themselves with actions of rival companies that deviate from current expectations. The projection of what competitors may do, how they may do it and why, will form a basis to this analysis. Scenario analysis is not making a series of predictions on what you believe will happen, it is making a series of projections about what may happen. The distinction between the two is very important because the purpose of the exercise is to highlight potential unprecedented scenarios. Past data and observation tells us what has happened in the past but it does not tell us what will happen in the future. This is a very important consideration with risk analysis because as I have already mentioned, risk is in the future not in past data. An assumption based on continuity will expose the investor to market shocks. Complacency in markets is a vital ingredient to asset price crashes and so one should always attempt to expect the unexpected by identifying a series of otherwise 'unexpected' scenarios which will identify weaknesses in the investor's holdings.

The Malthusian Trap

If you are new to the subject of economics, I would like to make very clear of the limitations in economic theory over the course of time as new developments can attenuate the application of particular theories. This necessitates adaption or discarding of said theories. An example of this being the Malthusian trap. In essence, this trap refers to a situation in which population growth is left unbridled and so will outperform growth in agricultural yields. In turn, leaving the economy in a position where resources are insufficient to meet demand. For obvious reasons this trap has better applicability to islands rather than large continents.

A case study was conducted on the populace of Easter Island which mirrored a dramatic boom and bust cycle. The empirical evidence leading to the coining of the 'Malthusian trap' being that the island's inhabitants exhausted the once abundant natural resources which led to the demise and total collapse of the local population. It has been found that the population grew and exceeded the carrying capacity of the island's resources. As the population expanded, the resources per capita fell. Consequently, beyond a certain threshold, the availability of natural resources acts as a limit for demographic growth. Unless population growth curtails accordingly; resource per capita reduces to a level that is below subsistence. The Malthusian trap provided an excellent explanation as to why Easter Island turned from a thriving province into a deserted isolated island.

Using these principles, several economists predicted that the population of the beautiful African island Mauritius would fall victim to the Malthusian trap leading it to a bleak future. Others challenged this forecast by stating that with an increase in population density, more people will generate new technologies which would avert Mauritius being confined to conditions within the trap. Indeed, Mauritius did avoid being trapped as the island's economic growth per capita managed to remain abreast with demographic development. It seems that population growth promoted efficiency and innovation. It is conceivable that technological advancements offset the factors that was used to predict the island becoming decadent.

On balance, then, a theory that adequately described the fate of Easter Island was proven incorrect when predicting a similar outcome for Mauritius. Prior to rendering this theory as redundant, one should question its applicability to the oil market. Having surpassed peak oil, much of the easy to access oil has been extracted and consumed. New discoveries are constrained by geography; the industry cannot find what simply is not there to be found. Production is constrained by politics; some governments may decide not to extract all of their oil reserves today and so may favor a strategy that gravitates towards thrift of reserves. It is equiprobable they may decide to increase production in the event that they favor selling more oil today at the expense of future sales.

Undeniably, in the absence of new technologies we are on course to dissipate the earth's oil reserves within the next generation. The Malthusian trap is a distinct reminder that as the earth's population grows, the oil per capita falls and an unsustainable situation looms. With the pressures this will place on net importing oil economies one must acknowledge that as with Mauritius, propensity to adapt and wean away from oil will increase as conditions deteriorate for net importers.

The Entitlement Culture

Governments tend to plan based on prior trends, it is rare for a government to plan using anything but an extrapolation of the past. For most of the Western economies, I believe that this has created an 'entitlements culture' in which promises of past were made on the assumption that the strong economic growth and boom times would be permanent. Yet we find ourselves in an environment of anemic economic growth, governments accruing unsustainable levels of debt and a voting public that expect entitlements of old to continue. The UK stood to gain from the industrial revolution, exporting large coal reserves, the discovery of oil in the North Sea and the introduction of consumer credit all leading to respective growth in GDP and tax receipts. In turn, allowing the government to implement and maintain projects like the National Health Service (NHS). However, the UK has recently transitioned from a net oil exporter to a net importer, cheap labor costs in Asia have led to the demise of the UK manufacturing industry as a global transition in manufacturing has shifted from west to east. The pressures from low labor Eastern workers has reduced the West's ability to demand pay increases of past and a firmly integrated economic rot is well established. And so we are presented with a dilemma – cut public expenditure to live within our means or continue as we are and accrue more debt. I tick the first postulate.

Prior to the first world war the pound dollar exchange rate valued the pound at 5 USD[33]. At the time of writing the pound is valued at 1.3 USD, in my view the pound falling below parity with the USD is a question of 'when', not 'if'. This points to a pessimistic view of the UK economy and with record amounts of tax payers funds being absorbed by the NHS one must question the sustainability of its provision. Keynesian economists will plausible highlight the link between the NHS and the multiplier effect. The NHS is a very large employer and the wages earned by NHS employees is used in the purchase of other goods and services within the economy. This resonates throughout the economy creating a ripple effect of indirect job creation. Having worked in the NHS I have seen firsthand the magnitude of misused and wasted resources which is perpetuating the current NHS crisis in the UK. I feel that the financial burden of this unfunded liability will only increase overtime if no changes are made. Moreover, the NHS is now catering for a larger and older population. It is ignorant to suggest that its problems can be rectified by throwing more and more money into its funding. The NHS needs reform – not a money tree.

For some time I have pontificated about the future of our NHS. I am perhaps not informed enough to make accurate predictions on this topic but I see two clear scenarios emerge. Either the NHS will continue in its current form which is underpinned by an ever increasing amount of tax revenues. Furthermore, there could be a small fee for using its services – much like an excess payment when claiming on an insurance policy. This could rid the system of some of the abuse that it incurs – people may think twice about going to hospital after vomiting if there is a £100 fee for doing so. Or, the provision of NHS services is tempered in a fashion that will encourage would-be patients to seek investigative procedures and operations in private facilities. If waiting lists are that extreme then people will consider their options. Should they opt for private treatment then the liability of funding will transfer from the government to the patient. Should a paradigm of this sort develop, I would not be surprised to see the government begin to partially subsidize private treatment as it will be economical for the state to part fund an operation in a private hospital - than to incur all costs by allowing the patient to be treated by the NHS. Such reneging on the initial 'from cradle to the grave' promise will not be popular with the public and so I believe any privatization will occur via the back door in a fashion not too dissimilar from that abovementioned.

The British public are passionate about the NHS but they often neglect to mention that in recent times its funding has been via loans from foreign governments. Owing to a gradual depletion of oil reserves and the abolishment of the Petroleum Revenue Tax (PRT), the North Sea Oil tax revenues that was a significant source of revenue is now severely dwindling. I wonder how this void will be filled within the economy. Which sector will offset the fall in revenue from a curtailing of oil reserves?

Great Britain does have a few aces up her sleeve, the English language is the third most spoken language and the most universally applied. Numerous empirical studies provide evidence that sharing a common language with a potential trading partner fosters propensity for bilateral trade. This is simple to envisage seeing as companies from either country will be able to communicate with each other - reducing the cost of trade. Intuitive to this, Britain should enjoy good relations with large export markets such as the USA and Canada. Post Brexit I imagine that tightening of these ties with said economies will be the focus of policy making and business decisions. Given that Great Britain is an isolated island with excellent transport links to many markets, this can be construe as an advantage as it has unrestricted access to the global market.

A brief mention of highly questionable subsidization of certain industries with tax payers funds is warranted because it could be construe as a retardation of growth. The elimination of PRT for oil producing companies operating in the UK continental shelve is a form of subsidizing these oil corporations and it has been estimated that the oil and gas industry may receive more in subsidies than it pays in taxes[34]. This translates simply into the UK taxpayer potentially funding foreign multinational corporations to extract oil from the UKCS which is a ridiculous notion. The UK Government have quoted job and energy security as well as balance of payments in justifying this policy but it demonstrates misallocation of capital and the sort of interventionism that has done more harm than good. I would never have voted for it, that's for sure.

Debt – an Economic Perspective

Debt has become a focal point of discussions within the investment community. This should come as no surprise given the well-publicized incidents involving Greece and Italian banks. From past observation, episodes of high leverage have been associated with subpar economic growth. The incidence of low interest rates also change the dynamics of the system where debt is concerned. Exceptionally high leverage ratios can protract for longer than usual under extended low real interest rates which summarizes the current climate. If credit grows faster than GDP then you have an increase in leverage – rising leverage will likely lead to a crisis and post-crisis recession.

Much has been said in regards to central banks printing currency to erode the real burden of debts through inflation. This argument has its merits, after all, periods of high indebtedness has historically been associated with episodes of high inflationary crises. In simplistic terms, a highly leveraged government will duly lead to higher taxes in the future, not forgetting that inflation is also a tax. Alternatively there could be a reduction in future government spending in an attempt to repay its debt. This reduction in spending will not be popular with voters - leaving the most probable outcome one in which expansion of the money supply is favored.

When concerned with household leverage, it is important to distinguish between the types of debt within the economy as increasing debt is often tarnished as a negative development, however, this is far from certain for the following reason. Debt is, by nature, a mechanism of bringing forward consumption. It's a vehicle for spending tomorrow's income today. Whether this be via loans or credit agreements; the western world cannot get enough of it. If you go to your local bank and take out a £20,000 loan and use it to treat yourself to some fancy clothes, games consoles, new laptop and a holiday to the Caribbean this is deemed as unproductive debt. Once the money is spent it is gone and it becomes a future liability as the principle needs to be outlaid to the creditor. If, say, I went into the bank and asked for the same loan agreement but used it to help convert an old garage into a functional car mechanics facility to be leased to a small business; this would be classified as productive debt. The purpose of the debt contract being to generate a future income and this type of debt should be deemed as positive for the economy.

It's this differentiation that is important as it is not the gross debt in the system that dictates how much consumers are binging tomorrows income today, it is what the funds borrowed are being allocated towards. I have little doubt that a period of high inflation will occur and reduce the real burden on debtors; which effectively will reward households that are highly geared with large mortgages during the disinflation that the most recent decade has given to us. This is particularly so for households that negotiated fixed interest rates on their mortgages.

Any increase in the published figures on consumer borrowing is often interpreted as a sign of confidence within the economy. Households are confident about the future and their future earnings being secure enough to justify spending forthcoming income today. Again, this is not a foregone conclusion as an increase in consumer borrowing can be done so as a matter of recourse in order to make ends meet. As the abovementioned account shows, it is dangerous to make broad assumptions on debt or consumer borrowing. Generalizations in the media on consumer leverage should not be taken too seriously unless the data is proven to suggest otherwise.

A fundamental flaw in zero-lower bound interest rates is that credit in advanced economies has been used to purchase already existing assets such as housing. This provides explanation as to how fiscal policies have done little to stimulate economic growth. Even if credit is being funneled to productive enterprises - emerging economies time and time again have demonstrated how this can produce waste with the so-called 'bridges to nowhere' projects.

Since the 2008 crisis, the endeavors of the western governments have only achieved a shift in debt from the private to the public sector rather than reduce it. During a post-crisis recession over leveraged households typically curtail consumption in favor of repaying debt. This leads to a reduction in demand within the economy. To offset this governments will operate fiscal deficits to rekindle growth, filling the void that the private sector has made. As households and businesses reduce their leverage – government balance sheets deteriorate and in the process the debt is not reduced but shifted. When market commentators talk of the large government debts one should remember that much of this originated in the private sector. The large scale deleveraging that we have seen since 2008 is further reasoning as to why the recovery has been so meagre and government debts have expanded so much. One must question to what degree does this practice become unsustainable.

In regards to the pockets of indebted Eurozone economies, the pain of austerity will be very burdensome for Greece. Its economy will not grow with the kind of budget that they will have to enact and in these conditions, their currency is way overvalued. Without the ability to grow - their ability to pay the interest and repay their debt will diminish. Similar fates await other weaker Eurozone countries such as Spain and Portugal. How long the ECB can postpone this inevitability by printing money is uncertain but these countries would be much better placed by reverting to their own respective currencies. If I was a native I would be campaigning for it.

Statistical Inference

Having studied statistics at degree level I have noted the underrepresentation of this subject in investment themed literature. There are several factors that warrant inclusion in any book that lays claim to assist the retail investor. Most importantly, I wish to make clear that data can be used to disprove a theory or assumption but never to prove one. For instance, I can collect a sample of adults from a given population and present the hypothesis that no adult human can exceed six feet in height. If my findings from the investigation show that none of my sample registered a height exceeding six foot it is insufficient to conclude that a human adult cannot exceed the predetermined height.

All that my study can do is provide evidence to support the hypothesis. However, if an individual was observed to be taller than six foot then my study could discredit the original hypothesis with overwhelming evidence – it would refute it. Secondly, much of the conclusions derived from data points within studies is possibly due to sample variance – this being natural variation between subjects that is sufficient to influence results. Other factors should also be considered such as whether the sample of subjects or data collected is a true reflection of the population from which it was taken, some results from studies are outright artefacts. Notwithstanding these points, economic theories are often rejected not necessarily as a derivative of a single conflicting result but more from a set of anomalous observations conjoined with the incidence of a better suited theory. One should not be fooled by a single study or observation when appraising investment opportunities.

The Rise of China

I previously wondered if the rise of China was another example of an economic bubble which would dwindle on its own accord. However, I now believe that the balance of economic power will continue to shift eastward and the west will continue to experience a reduction in living standards. Disposable income in the west has reduced primarily as a function of increased primary commodity prices due to the expansion of demand in the East. This forecast is underpinned by numerous fundamental developments. China in itself is a demographic powerhouse with just shy of 1.4 billion people. This eclipses the populace of the United States, Europe and the UK combined. Interestingly, outside of the USA China has the largest concentration of billionaires[35]. Commentators will often highlight that many manufacturing jobs in the US was lost to Chinese companies when in fact the data suggests that more jobs were lost to automation than offshoring.

China is an excellent reminder that the poverty trap stricken countries in Africa are not confined to a future of poverty. Countries can break out of these traps, we know this because otherwise we would all be poor. China is now very diversified – they have significant natural resource interest in Africa and have acquired many European corporations. It is difficult to see the advanced economies outperforming China in the next generation or two. Many commentators and books that centralize on the Chinese economy will speak of currency manipulation, cheap labor and deregulation as main contributors to the rise of China. I propose a new notion that China, if not by design then by accident, benefitted from a human capital dividend borne out from its one child policy.

China's Demographic Dividend

Households were fined and assets destroyed if they failed to comply with China's one child policy. In Chinese culture, parents rely on their children to support them in their old age. The more children a household has, the more support the parents can expect to receive when retired. If prior to the one child policy couples could raise three or four children, the implementation of the one child policy would undoubtedly ensure a marked reduction in financial support from their children.

This can be offset in two ways. A net increase in the saving ratio to compensate for the loss of future funds from children. Additionally, if a couple can only raise one child, then they will ensure that this child will be very highly educated; there is a quality versus quantity tradeoff with offspring. Parents could heavily invest in their single child to ensure that they have every opportunity to earn a high wage and contribute more. A highly educated workforce leads to a high labor productivity growth and so I believe that much of China's ability to break out of its poverty trap was a function of a high human capital only-child generation.

In my view, the rise of China will not be hampered by the US appointing protectionist policies and applying tariffs on Chinese goods. The exports of Taiwan and South Korea to China are more important than to the U.S. For Asian economies, exports to China is the key and Asia is much more interdependent with China than other markets like the US. China will undoubtedly encounter crisis of its own, the US had numerous depressions before becoming the superpower that it is today. I will not be reading too much into any crisis that China encounters over the next few decades. They are not averse to hard work and they are educating their young to a high standard, moreover, they do not have the unfunded liabilities that the West has. A recession or two will not stand in the way of the raging dragon.

Solar – a Bright Future?

One need not be a scientist to acknowledge that we are exhausting the earth's fossil fuel reserves. In the absence of rationing or technological advancement, it is possible that the oil reserves will be depleted in the next generation or two. Most of the easily accessible oil has been extracted and oil majors are committing to expensive exploration activities in some of the most remote provinces on earth in the search for new oil fields. When one considers the potential for growth in Asian populations it is foreseeable that the World's energy demand will soon be a multiple of what it is today. The per capita consumption of some of the poorest countries will increase with many of them purchasing vehicles for the first time. At today's oil price of $55/barrel I believe there is significant potential for much higher prices. The question remains: what will the world look like after the last barrel of oil is extracted?

From an economical perspective, one cannot refute both the advancement of the solar industry. It is perhaps paradoxical that wars are fought over oil fields yet we have the technology available to us to convert solar into usable energy. The cost of solar has reduced significantly for several reasons. Chiefly, the solar producing sector has profited from economies of scale and the learning curve. One of the earliest publications featuring the learning curve on electronic devices was conducted by Boston Consulting Group. They observed that when the production of electronic devices doubled, the marginal cost of producing subsequent units fell by twenty-five percent[36]. If the production of solar panels continues to expand then one would surmise that the marginal cost of production will continue to fall. A catalyst to cheaper solar has been an environment of low interest rates as solar farms have been able to raise capital at cheaper rates. This reduction in interest payments reduces the cost of electricity generation from solar farms. I believe, as with most things in technology, the efficiency of panels will increase. It is simple to see the future being smaller, more durable and powerful panels.

From an economical perspective, it is noteworthy that nuclear power generation is one of Solar's main rival technologies but it does not have the same advantage of marginal cost reduction from a learning curve. This is mainly as a result of each nuclear plant being constructed by different workers and so there is not the same efficiency promotion from repetition as seen with solar panels. The facility to benefit from 'learning by doing' is not as available as in the solar industry.

The very first solar cell was first invented in 1839 by Edmond Becquerel. Critics will argue that a technology that has been in existence for as long as this is still largely reliant on government subsidies. The retraction of these agreements may render the solar industry uncompetitive. My beliefs on this matter are simply that governments should reallocate the subsidies to support research and development of advancing the technology rather than underpin the industry in its current form. It is clear that solar is a viable solution to the impeding future oil supply crisis, however - suffice to say that the technology is still too futile at this time.

Western governments have publicly endorsed strategies to wean away from foreign oil dependency and so they have every incentive to develop existing solar technology. Additionally, the production of solar panels can occur in the lowest cost producing areas in the world such as China. However, if I was to instruct a local company to place panels on my roof manufacturing could occur anywhere in the world but the labor involved in the installation has to be local to where the technology is being deployed. Therefore the solar industry has a vital role in employment levels. Particularly so when most of jobs in the solar industry are in the design and installation of solar panel systems. In my view, any subsidy in solar is therefore a form of disguised fiscal stimulus that supports employment.

The higher the cost of fossil fuels, the greater the benefits of transitioning to solar energy. We are faced with a situation in which solar costs are falling and the conventional sources of energy production are increasing. Innovation is necessary for the sustainability of the solar industry and should be monitored with great interest.

Hope for the Future

I recently stood in a local book shop to review cover design ideas for this publication and noticed a very prominent trend with economics books. All seemed to relentlessly point to the problems with the World but I could not find one single book offering a solution or optimistic perspective. I was determined to venture my sense of how the global economy can be fixed.

Despite the obvious need for groundbreaking innovations – I believe that from an economist's perspective – the syllabus taught to budding economists needs significant reform. On my degree program there was endless models and formulas but not one mention of the Gold standard, the 1929 crash nor the Weimar crisis of 1923. I believe that this is a function of the shear arrogance of academics that the past is irrelevant as we have discovered the economic holy grail. We have so much trust in our models and policies that we can now control economic cycles and no matter what the markets throw at us, we can fix it. Why else would there be such little reference to once in a generation events that has shaped our world?

The Asian Financial crisis of the late 1990s, I believe, holds the solution on how to correct our mistakes and not pass a burden of debt and falling living standards to our grandchildren. The Asian Tigers became heavily dependent on foreign capital inflows and when the inevitable collapse came it was severe, spreading like wildfire between Asian economies. In November 1997 the contagion spread to Korea which subsequently suffered a currency and banking crisis. By the end of 1999 the Korean economy had rebounded rapidly and economic activity had surpassed its pre-crisis levels. So how did Korea do it?

The collapse of the Korean Won allowed for a rebalancing of imports and exports. As the Korean Won had collapsed - it made foreign imports expensive but goods produced domestically cheap for foreigners to purchase, boosting exports. As we know, this is not unique to Korea and is standard for any country involved in a currency crash. However, in early January 1998 there was an extraordinary public campaign in which households collected and donated their personal Gold inventories. Adults donated their jewelry and wedding rings whilst athletes gave up their medals. All of which was smelted into ingots to be sold to foreigners to pay down Korea's debts. Although this is an incredibly self-less gesture, it is not the solution that I am proposing for the Western hemisphere. It's the underlying capitulation and recognition that the party was over and now was the time to make sacrifices today for a better tomorrow.

Korea had realized it had lived beyond its means and was willing to do what was necessary to move on. Workers accepted significant pay reductions despite the Korean Won's depreciation and acknowledged that the way out of the crisis was to revert to hard work and living within one's means. Moreover, the Korean government had very little unfunded liabilities as only a small proportion of national income was allocated to pensions, unemployment benefits and state health provisions. Its lessons like the Asian contagion that should be consulted by policymakers when making decisions during crisis.

Sadly, I do not anticipate that any of the Western economies will replicate this togetherness that is required to prevent the impending implosion. The United Kingdom cannot afford her unfunded liabilities in their current form and is borrowing in an unsustainable fashion. The sooner we recognize that we cannot afford the expensive promises that we once made to ourselves - the more chance we have of averting a significant reduction of living standards.

My worry is that our governments will continue to use QE to inflate the real value of our debt away. Overtime this will equalize the exchange rates between East and West which will allow rich Asian companies and individuals to cherry-pick the West's best assets – this including prime real estate and companies. In effect we will be selling the family jewels to continue to maintain our standard of living. I believe that we need to reform the unfunded liabilities and revert back to a free-market system in which there is less control over monetary and fiscal policies.

We should accept that artificially reducing unemployment levels is not the road to prosperity and the market should be left to dictate economic conditions more than we are currently making allowances for. When you hold interest rates at zero lower bound in the manner that we have and run current account deficits for as long as we have you are making a deal with the devil for borrowed time. As we know all too well, these arrangements will never end well.

The Future of the Oil Market

The focus here will not be on specific oil price predictions but likely scenarios for the industry. Companies and countries with low production costs will likely look to maintain or increase output even if crude prices trend lower. This done so in the name of protecting their revenue and has been seen in countries that are dependent on oil exports. If the price of oil falls then more of it has to be extracted just to maintain the same level of income. If one wonders how low oil prices could go before the lower cost producers are no longer profitable then Iran's USD1.94 per barrel cost should act as a rough guide[37]. Many market commentators suggest that the solution should be to taper production so that prices can rise but I disagree with this suggestion. In 2016, Woodmac published a report stating that of the 79.7 million barrels of oil produced daily in the US, a mere 7.7 million barrels will be sold at a loss given an oil price as low as USD25/bbl[38].

The reluctance to invest in exploration activities due to current suppressed prices could lead to supply issues in the future which will duly rise prices in times to come. In response to the pressures on margins, oil extraction companies have embarked in cost-cutting exercises, the workforce being an easy target for this reduction in expenditure. Although an obvious strategy, we have seen in the past that dramatic cutting at the bottom of markets can affect the corporation's ability to respond when market conditions improve. Even resource rich corporations rely on sufficient levels of human capital.

Should oil prices remain at their current equilibrium levels it would not be a surprise to see a paradigm of mergers and acquisitions either in the interests of cash flow or under duress as higher cost companies struggle to adapt. Furthermore, oil majors may seize opportunities to acquire smaller companies at reasonable valuations at current prices. I have noted over the years in several sectors that mergers and acquisitions can be a sign that an economic downtrend is nearing its end. The oil services industry could see similar transitions, given the aggressive cost cutting seen in this sector it remains to be seen how well the industry will respond when conditions improve. Nevertheless, cash rich firms that are diversified in other sectors can seize opportunities to take over their smaller rivals that are highly geared to the energy sector to tap into their human capital resources and grow market share.

Any meaningful recovery in oil prices is likely to incentivize exploration activities in high risk environments. Oil and gas exploration has been taking place within the Arctic Circle for several decades, until recently this activity has been restricted to onshore or near-shore operations. There is no contention that the potential rewards of exploring the Arctic Circle are extremely lustrous. The Arctic continental shelf remains one of the last areas with unexplored potential for significant hydrocarbon reserves. Cash rich oil majors will likely be the first movers to exploit this prospect but given its harsh environment the artic continental shelve will not give up her resources easily.

With many rig operators opting for self-insurance, shareholders should be aware of the potential risks in tapping into unexplored harsh environments. The Deepwater Horizon Study Group concluded that since 1993, only 43 wells drilled were as complex as BP's Macondo well[39]. One could surmise that based on this data there is an approximate one in forty-three chance of a similar incident occurring based on past data alone. Yet there are many more factors to be considered before we accept such assumptions.

The fallacies in human risk calculation shows that under the hindsight bias, it is likely that many will attribute the 'well from hell' as being an outlier that could not possibly affect their own company. The longer the absence of similar events the more this belief will be reinforced. Time will tell on this matter but I am expecting to switch the news on one day to see another major well blowout. If asked to predict the future price of oil I would say that this depends almost entirely on only a few isolated factors. Firstly, the intensity of money printing by the Federal Reserve and secondly – the economic growth of China and India. In the event of aggressive expansionary monetary policies by the central banks then oil prices could go ballistic as they did in the wake of the 2008 financial crisis. Secondly, to illustrate the significance of Chinese and Indian economic growth on the future demand of oil some brief analysis will be performed.

In accordance with data published by the Central intelligence Agency and British Petroleum – the following statistics have been computed. In the interests of accuracy, these figures are correct to two decimal places. The current per capita consumption of crude oil for the USA is 21.85 barrels per day (bbl/d), the UK's is 8.82 bbl/d and France's is 8.77 bbl/d[40]. The US is evidently an outlier from a sample of countries that has not been included in this analysis – presumably, inter alia, owing to the vast dispersion of the geographic area in the US.

Interestingly, China and India have a per capital bbl/d consumption of 3.18 and 1.2 respectively. Owing to the fact that China's population is ~1,373,541,278[41] and India's ~1,266,883,598[42]. If one accepts that the per capita consumption of oil will begin to convergence between India, China and the Western Economies – then a transformational shift in the oil market is set to transpire within the next decade or two. It is simple to see how economic growth will lead to a rise of incidence in the number of Indians purchasing a car for the first time and an increase in aviation traffic and transportation of goods. Unless supply can be adjusted to offset this, then in the absence of a breakthrough in an alternative to oil - there is little other feasible scenario to oil prices increasing exponentially. Should this situation materialize – there will be intense growth in energy conservational technologies and also a significant wealth generation in oil exporting economies.

Graphene

Whilst researching the advancements in solar technology I stumbled across reports on a substance called Graphene. The substance was discovered in 2004 in a British University, the two scientists were later rewarded with a Nobel prize for their groundbreaking work. I believe, with my limited scientific knowledge, that graphene has the potential to redefine many of the everyday instruments that we use. Put simply, Graphene could one day change our World. It also has the potential to develop into a market that could become an economic bubble much like the internet stocks did at the turn of the millennium. The properties of graphene are so unique that technology giants are investing heavily in various graphene patents.

Graphene is the thinnest known material in the universe and the strongest ever measured, making it thinner than paper yet stronger than steel. It is elastic and can stretch up to 20% of its length. It is a very efficient electrical conductor and at room temperature it can sustain electric currents in far excess than that of copper[43]. The main focus of graphene deployment is gravitating towards the smart technology market. I am confident that significant wealth will be generated from this new innovation as scientists learn how to develop its applicability into other markets and products. The potential disruption to current technology by Graphene may be some years off yet but it is difficult to see a situation whereby an invention with these superior qualities is squandered and not integrated into many of our everyday products.

How the West can be saved

As an economist, it is clear to me that our incumbent governments cannot continue to underpin demand by spending monies borrowed from abroad. There must be a change of tact to allow the economy to become more self-sufficient. I believe that the level of inequality within the economy is acting as a retardant on growth for the following reasons. In a globalized setting where there is mobility of capital – many firms will locate in jurisdictions offering the most attractive tax rates. This can incentivize governments to enter a 'race to the bottom' in lowering corporation tax rates to attract foreign entities. Invariably these depressed rates can lead to a reduction in government revenue which would have otherwise funded liabilities such as education programs. If this results in a scaling of budgets then it is simple to see how underfunded establishments can lead to a lower standard of graduates. School leavers are an investment as an ageing population becomes increasingly dependent on the next generation's productivity for their essential provisions such as the National Health Service.

A by-product of excessive wealth is the concentration of power and this can be used to influence those in governments to act in the wealthy's best interests. If the rich can influence economic policy then the government may act in the best interests of a select few rather than that of the majority. However, the main justification for governments to target inequality is that distributing wealth from the bottom to the top reduces demand. As I will explain, the highest earners are the ones that dictate capital spending. It is this group that create jobs and so their place in society is important but one should consider that a high concentration of wealth amongst the few results in pockets of wealth and accumulation of idle capital. It is well documented that poor households spend all their income whereas the wealthy tend to only spend a small proportion of theirs. Therefore, if much of the increase in living standards is experienced by those at the top, arguably, less is being spent in domestic businesses. Give a poor household £100 and that money will be quickly outlaid as they use it for basic sustenance. Give £100 to a millionaire and there is every chance that it is invested abroad or left in a bank account. This simple thought experiment highlights the importance of ushering capital to the agents that will make best use of it to prop up domestic demand. I contest that funneling capital to the top is not going to sustain consumption in a way that can underpin employment for excessive periods.

Governments are important redistribution vehicles in which market failures can be corrected. If capital is being horded by the wealthy then only the government can interpose to reallocate the capital in a fashion that will benefit the wider demographic. If the markets are left unfettered then divergences in wealth will continue and aggregate demand within the economy can be markedly lower than its potential. Some market commentators may disagree with this perception by claiming that GDP per capita increases show that the economy is moving forward. The issue with this view is that GDP per capita can be skewed by outliers. If there was a sudden influx of billionaires relocating to St Kitts then the GDP per capita would duly increase but the average resident has not become wealthier. Therefore, rising GDP per capita can be the product of an increase in inequality.

Given that central banks have reduced base rates to zero-lower bound and engaged in quantitative easing programs - many investors fear that the mechanisms to remedy the anemic growth have already been exhausted. This is not the case as policies that reduce the extremes of inequality will act as a stimulus to aggregate demand. Taxation policies should look to redistribute some wealth which will then be spent within the economy to increase consumption. Allowing the rich to continue to accumulate capital will likely do little to stimulate the economy beyond what has already been seen – we know this as we have experienced this paradigm since 2008 yet many households report a fall in disposable income.

Therefore, on balance of this evidence, I believe that the next growth catalyst could be the reduction in some of the inequality which has been fostered under the conditions made by the zero-lower bound interest rates and government inertia. The recommendations of this book are not to equalize equality as financial incentives are very important drivers for growth but policies that act as vehicles to transfer some of the excessive wealth held by the super-rich into the everyday household should be encouraged. Previously, many have seen that an aggressive tax system that redistributed wealth from top to bottom takes from the productive to give to the unproductive but many now see the benefit of preventing pockets of wealth within an economy in the view of increasing overall consumption. The challenge becomes finding a government that is centralist enough to allow profiteering that encourages entrepreneurs to take risks and invest in the economy but leftist enough to temper the vast wealth accumulation by the super-rich in society. Achieving this will place money in the hands of the masses and should prove a potent stimulus to the economy. Perhaps it is appropriate to conclude this section by sharing a quotation that I recently found by a former chairman of the Federal Reserve.

'A giant suction pump had by 1929 to 1930 drawn into a few hands an increasing proportion of currently produced wealth. This served them as capital accumulations. But by taking purchasing power out of the hands of mass consumers, the savers denied themselves the kind of effective demand for their products which would justify reinvestment of the capital accumulation in new plants.

In consequence as in a poker game where the chips were concentrated in fewer and fewer hands, the other fellows could stay in the game only by borrowing. When the credit ran out, the game stopped'. - Mariner Eccles (Chairman of the Federal Reserve, 1951)[44].

Our Future World

The media and many market analysts hold predictive forecasts in high regard, too high if the truth be known. I seldom take too much notice of any of these projections as in our complex world - one single development can change the course of the global economy which is why I dedicate little effort in trying to predict the future. Any projection is subject to correction upon submission of further information and so I encourage the reader to take very little notice of politicians, central bankers or company reports that forecast along trajectories into the future. With good fortune the reader of this book will have noted the difficulties in analyzing markets and recognized the importance of portfolio diversification. I share many of the views of the bears when evaluating the prospects of the western world. However, there are many paths that can steer us away from the seemingly inevitable wealth transfer from west to east.

Reform on the unfunded liabilities and less intervention will be an excellent start. Astutely following the developments in key markets such as China and India will dictate which businesses thrive and which do not. These markets will offer astronomical sources of demand in the next generation. In any case, the Western investor should ensure adequate diversification at all times – no matter how confident they are on a given prospect, no one knows for sure how the world will be in several years from now. No matter how dire the global outlook seems - capital will search for yield and so there will always be a bull market somewhere in the world, one must not put all of their eggs into one single basket trying to find it though.

In terms of the debt situation, it is correct to suggest that for a pound to be borrowed there must have been a pound saved elsewhere. Therefore, the sum of all of the world's liabilities and assets will always sum to zero. Keynesian economists will iterate that the overall level of debt will not make a difference because one person's debt is another person's assets. Perhaps these people should explain this to the Greeks. Crisis will occur through the imbalance of savings and debts. Countries that save too much will allow for other countries to borrow excessively and unsustainably. Many ascribe the housing market bubble of 2008 to the excessive saving activities of China which depressed the interest rates and allowed for excessive capital to flow into the housing market.

The US, in my view, will continue to adopt expansionary monetary policies in order to monetize their debts and hold interest rates below that of inflation. These policies will undoubtedly have a negative effect on the value of the US Dollar. This said, other currencies may also depreciate and possibly at a faster rate to the US Dollar; but the US Dollar will depreciate against something. As aforementioned, I am very cautious about making long term predictions because forecasting is a dynamic and not static process. One single event can throw an economy off course and so new developments will require multiple iterations. This said, I am certain that unless the US and other Western economies can reverse their current account deficits, the central banks will rely on printing new currency to release the burden of current debts. You will observe momentum in Eastern companies and individuals buying assets in the West – that I am certain of.

The feasible alternative scenario is a global demand boom which causes a surge in output and allows for western governments to paydown proportions of their debts. The key to this will probably be innovation or rising per capita income of the emerging economies. The vast demographic of the emerging economy populous means a small raise in per capita income may only be a marginal improvement on an individual level but when you consider the magnitude of the wealth that will be created in these poor countries you can see how a demand boom could materialize. Even a small marginal per capita income will be a gigantic increase in wealth owing to the magnitude of these markets.

It comes as a surprise to me that the possibility of an inflationary crisis is seldom mentioned by market commentators or economists. According to official CPI data, since the early 1990s inflation has been well contained within the UK. This is in part attributed to the offshoring activities and investment in automation. These have their limitations and I would not exclude a reunion with our old friend – high consumer price inflation. As already discussed, the central banks will be restricted in their efforts to starve inflation using the traditional interest rate mechanism due to the leverage of the private and public sectors. It is simple to see how exposed our economies are to an inflationary crisis. If I had to make predictions on the global economy a high incidence of inflation would be one of my foremost thoughts given the potential for newly created capital to flow into consumer goods markets. A catalyst for this may be legislation for increases in the minimum wage but there are many other factors that will also contribute.

I believe that western governments need to capitulate on their unfunded liability programs that are indebting our future generations and concentrate on productivity of their domiciliary firms. I do not believe that protectionism, as endorsed by the European Union, is a path to prosperity. Forming trading blocs like the EU may promote self-trade within the bloc but there is a danger that trade relations may deteriorate between trade blocs. Protectionism provides a pardon to firms that are inefficient and will not lead to better economic conditions.

As aforementioned, the short-termism of government parties in power will prolong any necessary privatization or reform of bodies such as the NHS which is proving to be burdensome on the weakened national balance sheets. I believe that privatization is the last resort to solving any NHS crisis. Reduction of inefficiencies such as penalizing abusers of this free service can be progressed further than it currently is but this is an emotive subject. As previously proposed, a potential solution could be that when an individual wishes to visit an accident and emergency department they are charged a small fee, much like an excess payment when claiming on an insurance policy. The leftwing politicians will claim this will impact the poorest in society and I agree, but it will make some service users take more responsibility prior to abusing the NHS and reduce some of the unnecessary strain on the system. Otherwise the UK will see a marked increase in their taxes to fund this inefficient entity.

Many market commentators were bearish on UK property in the 1990s, whilst their analysis and argument had merit, they underestimated the interventionalist attitude of the Bank of England in expanding the money supply which propelled property prices upwards for well in excess of a decade. It is possible that central banks continue to support asset markets by continuing to print currency and maintain negative real interest rates.

Fiscal and monetary policies have achieved one thing, they have reduced the frequency of recessions but when recessions do occur they are much more potent than those of past. Attempting to tame the beast of economic cycles will not end well. We have created an environment where capital has pushed asset prices up exponentially and there is a potent risk of an asset price deflation scenario which could be the source of a future financial crisis. These crashes will occur as a byproduct of imbalances, with so many imbalances and disequilibrium's it can be near on impossible to accurately predict an impending crisis but I want to make it very clear that asset price deflation is a real threat to our economy. Black Swan events of this type occur because they are unexpectable and so informed diversification should always be practiced when investing, this involves diversifying asset purchases and also the timing of asset purchases. Far too many investors fail to recognize that a form of diversification is sporadic purchasing of assets.

The means to remedy the issue of inequality is not as obvious as one may hope. The tax system is a redistribution mechanism as by taxing a household's income it can be reallocated to others via welfare payments. Progressive tax policies which feature a rise in the proportion of a worker's salary being paid in tax increases linearly with rises in their income. At first glance it is plausible that this may seem an obvious choice in reducing inequality. It is important to realize that wealth typically has greater inequality than salaries. The government should not interpose too much in the labor market because it may cause despondency amongst the higher paid individuals whom may choose to become less productive as large proportions of any salary increases are relinquished to the tax man. Under this system, it is simple to see how valuable human capital may wish to take early retirement and cause efficiency to deteriorate. Political parties that approach the electorate and state that they will go after the highest percentage of income earners will gain popularity for sure, however, this is not a good economic strategy as the decision makers on capital spending is often the higher earners – not the income earners working in department stores.

Perhaps a better solution would be to tax wealthy landlords that enrich themselves in the buy-to-let property market. More could be done to restrict these property investors sitting on goldmine nest eggs at the expense of young adults that are raising young families in their own parent's houses as they are unable to move onto the property ladder. Ending some of the inefficient subsidies seen in the UK will also lessen the future burden on taxpayers.

I have generally refrained from disclosing too many specific predictions for reasons already mentioned. However, what good is economic knowledge if one does not have an opinion on future investment themes? I accept that one single event may negate any suggestions that is offered here. After all, even John Keynes once quoted 'when the facts change, I change my mind. What do you do, sir?'. This is notwithstanding the fact that from time to time markets do present opportunities to profit from analysts that adopt a contrarian perspective. For instance, on the eve of Brexit the pound had been steadily inclining against many other major currencies. During a televised interview a commentator suggested that there was record representation of individuals from council estates voting in the EU referendum. It struck me that these individuals were likely to vote in favor of Brexit and the market had already priced in a 'Remain' result. I acknowledged the chance of a 'leave' vote being more probable than then market valuations were suggesting.

I purchased several ounces of Gold prior to the first results being announced. When alleged 'remain' strongholds were weaker than expected - the pound started to fall against Gold and the US Dollar. Throughout the night more results were announced causing the pound to tank against Gold and the Dollar. The decision to reduce my exposure to my own currency was an immediately profitable one but it is rare to see markets present such obvious opportunities as they did on the eve of Brexit. Usually I would be contempt that my portfolio is diversified enough to withstand any rare event and so I would not adjust my position based on an alleged opportunity to make a quick profit. It is difficult beating the professionals at their own game and many will lose fortunes attempting it.

My logic can be extended to the current situation in Greece. If I was a Greek citizen I would be making use of the Euro's strength to cumulatively buy physical Gold, foreign equities and property. The Greek economy is far too weak to withstand the strong Euro currency over the longer-term and so the situation in Greece, on balance, suggests that Greece will one day readopt its own currency which will duly devalue markedly against the Euro. This will reboot the Greek economy but the middle class will bear the brunt of losses caused by the exchange rate revaluation. If this hypothesis is proven correct then Greek investors can preserve any wealth that they have by exposing themselves to markets that cannot be effected by local currency denominated assets depreciating.

If reducing inequality is the key to increased future prosperity then I suggest that there will always be divergences of opinion on such emotive issues such as inequality. If one accepts that economies that are more equal grow better, then one must question whether the existing inequality between the developed world and emerging economies is not reducing global growth. If the West does realize a reduction in living standards then a global convergence will be inevitable. This could be a blessing in disguise.

As a final note to investors: one must not obsess over historic nominal valuations of assets as these are only an indicator. We should not exclusively gauge the value of a share by its nominal price in domestic currency. One should instead consider appraising it by other means such as in a foreign currency, precious metals or barrels of oil. This is because the domestic currency is a variable that is subject to market forces. People think of the pound as a fixed constant but it is actually an unstable asset and is constantly changing. A £50 note will always be a £50 note but the purchasing power of the note will constantly fluctuate and this will have an impact on investment valuations.

When an investor reviews historical share price movements they are seeing the product of the supply and demand of the individual equity as well as that of the currency – both factors impact the share price. If a currency is revalued it will be reflected in the share price. After the UK's EU referendum vote the pound fell against a range of currencies. Many pound denominated shares increased thereafter giving the impression that the valuations were now more expensive but this was a mere adjustment to offset the lower value of the pound. The pound prior to the UK's 'Leave' vote was not the same pound after as it was a much weaker currency. Always consider the fluctuating nature of a currency's purchasing power when making investment decisions.

In sum, experience shows that each crisis unveils a new set of risks. Old risks can manifest themselves in different forms, making it increasingly difficult to predict the cause and timing of the next crisis. Particularly so in a world where there is more information available to us than we know how to use. Governments that practice interventionalist measures may be compounding the problem due to their myopic attitudes and desire to protract unsustainable unfunded liability programs. Inflating asset markets is certainly not the solution to the West's problems but it has allowed us to postpone many of our deep-rooted problems. However, the investor must adapt to the state of global affairs and despite the that the past cannot predict the future, one must recognize that because human nature seldom changes overtime – whilst history may not repeat – every now and then it rhymes.

.

REFERENCES

1. Bresciani, T. (2006). The economics of Inflation – A study of post War Germany
2. Waring, A. (1998) Managing Risk. South-Western Cengage Learning. London, UK.
3. Business Insider, (2011) Hong Kong Property: Did You See The Crash Coming In 1997? Available at: http://www.businessinsider.com/hong-kong-property-did-you-see-the-crash-coming-in-1997-2011-6?IR=T (Accessed 23 November 2016).
4. Monnery, N. (2011) Safe as Houses? London Publishing Partnership, London. United Kingdom
5. OECD (2000) Competition and Regulation Issues in the Pharmaceutical Industry.
6. Malhota, P. Impact of TRIPS in India (2010) CPI Anthony Rowe, Chippenham and Eastborne. United Kingdom
7. Sprenger, C. (2008) State Owned Enterprises In Russia. ICEF, Higher School of Economics, Moscow, Russia.
8. 'The Active Economist' (2015). Available at: https://activeeconomist.wordpress.com/2015/02/14/hyperinflation-in-zimbabwe/ (accessed 12 Febraury 2017).
9. BBC Website (2008), Zimbabwe inflation spirals again. Available at: http://news.bbc.co.uk/1/hi/business/7244769.stm (Accessed 12 February 2017)
10. Washington State University Magazine (2008) Available at: http://wsm.wsu.edu/researcher/wsmaug11_billions.pdf Accessed 9 February 2017
11. The International Bank for Reconstruction and Development/The World Bank (2011) Demand-Led Transformation of the Livestock Sector in India. Washington, USA
12. BBC Website. (2012) Meet the UK's oldest Farmers, Available at: http://www.bbc.co.uk/news/magazine-17537153 (Accessed 13 January 2017)
13. Waring, A. (1998) Managing Risk. South-Western Cengage Learning. London, UK.

14. European Central Bank, Available at: https://www.ecb.europa.eu/ecb/tasks/international/emerging/html/index.en.html (Accessed November 2016)
15. World Development Report 2009: Reshaping Economic Geography. World Bank (2009) p.101
16. Central Intelligence Agency – The World Factbook. Available at: https://www.cia.gov/library/publications/the-world-factbook/fields/2177.html (Accessed August 2016)
17. Venas News (2016) Richest President in Africa with a net worth $20 billion- Jose Eduardo dos Santos. Available at: https://venasnews.co.ke/2016/07/11/richest-president-africa-net-worth-20-billion-jose-eduardo-dos-santos/
18. The World Bank. (Undated) Available at: http://data.worldbank.org/country/angola
19. Africa Ranking. The Richest Presidents in Africa. Available at: http://www.africaranking.com/richest-presidents-in-africa/ (Accessed September 2016)
20. National Bureau Of Economic Research, (2008). Capital Flow Bonanzas: An Encompassing View Of The Past And Present
21. The Telegraph, (2017) Black Wednesday: The moment power shifted to the markets. Available at: http://www.telegraph.co.uk/finance/economics/9542130/Black-Wednesday-The-moment-power-shifted-to-the-markets.html (March 2017)
22. The Telegraph, (2016). Rolls-Royce set to reveal £2bn write-down as sterling's plunge weighs. Available at: http://www.telegraph.co.uk/business/2016/07/23/rolls-royce-set-to-reveal-2bn-write-down-as-sterlings-plunge-wei/ (Accessed December 2016)
23. Building Codes Illustrated. Ching. F (2007) John Wiley & Sons
24. Kahneman, D., & Tversky, A. (1979). Prospect theory: An analysis of decision under risk. *Econometrica, 47*, 263-291.
25. French, D. (2010) Walk Away: The rise and fall of the homeownership myth. Ludwig von Mises Institute, Alabama, USA
26. BP 2016 Annual Report, Available at: https://www.bp.com/content/dam/bp/en/corporate/

pdf/investors/bp-annual-report-and-form-20f-2016.pdf
27. BBC News, (2013) Tesco Profits Fall as Supermarket Pulls Out Of US. Available at: http://www.bbc.co.uk/news/business-22179255 (Accessed April 2016)
28. Fosback, N (1985) Stock Market Logic, Fort Lauderdale, Florida. Institute for Econometric Research
29. BBC News, (2013) Tesco Profits Fall as Supermarket Pulls Out Of US. Available at: http://www.bbc.co.uk/news/business-22179255 (Accessed April 2016)
30. Accountants For Business (2010) Risk and Reward: Tempering the Pursuit of Profit. London, United Kingdom
31. Economist Intelligence Unit (2005) Reputation: risk of risks, London. United Kingdom
32. Cowton, Christopher J. (2009) Accountingand the ethics challenge: Re-membering the professional body. Accounting and Business Research. P177-190 The Telegraph (2016) From $5 to $1.22: the 200-year journey of the pound against the dollar Available at: http://www.telegraph.co.uk/money/special-reports/from-5-to-122-the-200-year-journey-of-the-pound-against-the-doll/ (Accessed July 2016)
33. Offshore Oil Offshore Tax (2016) A case study of Chevron's North Sea Operations. International Transport Workers Federation, Sydney, Australia.
34. Tse, E. (2015) China's Disruptors. Clays Ltd, St Ives Plc, United Kingdom
35. Stern, C.W. and Stalk, G. Jr (1998) "Perspectives on Strategy: From the Boston Consulting Group", John Wiley & Sons
36. Wall Street Journal (2016) Barrel Breakdown. Available at: http://graphics.wsj.com/oil-barrel-breakdown/
37. Wood Mackenzie (2016) Oil Prices – production shut-ins and the cost curve. Available at: https://www.woodmac.com/content/portal/energy/highlights/wk1__15/Wood%20Mackenzie_oil_prices_production_shut_ins_and_the_cost_curve%20Feb%202016.pdf?webSyncID=b8a7e3f4-bff2-4036-8ff8-2a885f34fe63&sessionGUID=c4c6c7eb-6e49-42e4-8049-31161a316afe
38. Maastricht European Institute for Transnational Legal Research, (2014) **Civil Liability and Financial Security for Offshore Oil and Gas Activities** Available at:

http://ec.europa.eu/dgs/energy/tenders/doc/2013/20131028_b3-978-1_final_report.pdf (Accessed March 2017)

39. British Petroleum (2016) Bp statistical Review June 2016. Available at: https://www.bp.com/content/dam/bp/pdf/energy-economics/statistical-review-2016/bp-statistical-review-of-world-energy-2016-full-report.pdf
40. Central Intelligence Agency. Available at: https://www.cia.gov/library/publications/the-world-factbook/geos/ch.html
41. Central Intelligence Agency. Available at: https://www.cia.gov/library/publications/the-world-factbook/geos/in.html
42. The Conversation, (2012) Harder than diamond, stronger than steel, super conductor … graphene's unreal. Available at: http://theconversation.com/harder-than-diamond-stronger-than-steel-super-conductor-graphenes-unreal-5123
43. R.Skidelsky (2011) 'The relevence of Keynes' p.11. Cambridge Journal of Economics. Oxford University Press.

INDEX

Africa: 178, 179
    -demographic 81
    -landlock 78,79
    - Mauritius 168

Agriculture 69, 70
    -Commodities 57, 60
    -Supply 71, 167

Asia: 180, 187
    -crisis 106, 185, 186

Black Swan: 52, 139, 140, 144, 200
    -insurance 141, 142

China: 71, 72, 153, 178, 179, 180, 183, 191, 195, 196
    -demographic 179, 192
    -gold 104

Currency: 52, 63, 65, 67, 92
    - Euro 67
    - Pegs 95, 96, 97, 98, 111, 137

Decisional Bias 126, 129, 130
    -hindsight 190
    - survivorship 105, 133
    - confirmation 135

Dividend: 104, 107
    -cover 112, 113
    -demographic 81, 82, 179
    -reinvestment 111

Equilibrium: 17, 31
    -employment 26, 33
    - interest rate 36
    -oil 189
    -output 51

Gold: 95, 103-107, 199
    -Brown's Bottom 165
    -Brexit 202, 203
    -House Prices 37
    -standard 68
    -substitution 60

Greece: 67
  -Debt 174, 203, 204

Human Capital: 64, 77, 79, 80, 84

India: 191, 192, 195

Innovation: 193, 196
  -Risk 156, 157
  -Solar 184

Lindy Effect: 47, 48, 49

Monopoly: 40, 41, 43, 44, 46
  -Patents 45
  -Pharmaceutical 40, 41, 42

Nationalization 121
  -Banks 123

Oil: 40, 55, 57, 88, 111, 148, 168-173, 181, 183, 188-192
  -crash 37
  -fields 57, 58, 90
  -see black swan
  -see Dutch disease

Property- 30, 32, 33, 114, 201, 203
  -UK 199

Protectionism: 76, 106, 180, 198
  -Japan 18

Solar: 61, 181, 182, 183, 184
  -see Lindy Effect

Tariffs: 74, 75, 51
  -china 106, 180
  -see protectionism

Tesco: 145, 150, 154, 160

US Dollar: 58, 88, 170, 188

Zimbabwe: 50, 52, 81, 88, 99

ABOUT THE AUTHOR

Levi Donohoe from Chatham, England. Studied BSc Economics & Mathematics and MSc Financial Risk Management. A keen investor and Investment Analyst based in London, United Kingdom.

www.ingramcontent.com/pod-product-compliance
Lightning Source LLC
Chambersburg PA
CBHW020902180526
45163CB00007B/2595